Trust, Trust, Trust

How To Trust The Father, Son & Holy Spirit

Candace B. Franklin

Published by Word Therapy Publishing

September 23, 2020

ISBN-13: 978-0-9755163-9-3

Printed in the United States of America all rights reserved under international Copyright laws.

Cover Design by: Aspen Denita

Word Therapy Publishing, LLC

P.O. Box 939

Hope Mills, NC 28348

www.wordtherapypublishing.com

Dedication

This book is dedicated to the loving memory of my God-brother, **Raymond Silance Riley** who walked a courageous fight against the condition named ALS (Amyotrophic Lateral Sclerosis) also known as Lou Gehrig's disease and walked by faith into the arms of ALS (A Loving Savior). ALS is a disorder that affects the function of nerves and muscles. Raymond's life exemplified his love for God through his love for his wife, his mother and for his family. Raymond's journey bears witness that God loves us all and how He wants an intimate relationship with us, when we let Him in. Raymond walked with courage and admitted that it was okay to be scared, but not to walk in the spirit of fear. We thank God that we were a part of that journey knowing that Raymond remains forever in our hearts.

Foreword by Randy & Candace

If it had not been for the Lord on our side, where would we be? It was the grace of God that allowed us to walk through the valley of shadow of death, as we feared no evil, by Trusting God. It was truly trusting God that gave us daily strength to walk through a three-year storm. We give God ALL the Glory! We thank God for our beautiful family, Tyler, Chris and Seth and it is our collective prayer that by sharing our pain and victory; this book will allow many to be set free, redeemed and delivered.

Prayer

Lord we humbly come to you, giving you thanks. Let the words written in this book and the meditation of my heart be acceptable in thy sight, my Lord, my Strength, and my Redeemer. Lord, let every heart that is hard become soft, change our attitudes, change our outlook, and touch each one so that our lives will be changed forever more. Let your people receive the power of your anointing. Lord, let the power of the Holy Spirit be released in this book to declare your glory. Lord, we take authority over every demonic spirit and any plots or plans that would hinder your word from coming forth. Let your word be unhindered and uninterrupted. Let us walk in our divine purpose. In Jesus Name, we pray Amen.

Table of Contents

Chapter 1:
Go Through To Get To

All my life, beginning with my earliest memory from childhood, even as a little girl, I was always drawn to babies and toddlers. As I grew older my love for children grew along with me. I would pick them out in crowded areas, such as riding on push packed NYC buses and subways during my travels within the busiest city limits. My draw, my love and my focus soon developed itself into a genuine concern for the well-being of each child that I encountered. I did not understand it at the time, but God was shaping my heart for my future.

I remember crying at night for a child who was moving away. Oh, how that loss deeply affected me. When others were sad for the moment, I cared for them still in my heart long after their departure. My attachment was not to be unexplained. I remembered there was a picture of a little African girl who had a cinnamon colored face with real big beautiful sweet and loving eyes that hung in my childhood one -bedroom apartment. She was African, noted by her ancestral clothing as well as her hair style and its short coarse texture. She literally became the backdrop of my landscape and in my heart. I gazed into her eyes daily wondering who she was and what her life was like. I grew to love her without a cause. Her eyes showed endearment and plain ole love. It seemed like her eyes were the mirror to her soul. Without me realizing it, I was searching for my own identity. The questions that I pondered internally soon were lived out daily. I began my life's quest to find out who indeed Candace Anita Bright (back then) was to become.

During one of our talks, God reminded me of my unspoken prayers. He heard me and answered. I asked God at the age of 9, "Will I one day be a Mommy?" So there starts my journey with children. Little did I know that I would become a Mother, a Mentor, a Guidance Counselor, a Confidant and listening ear to both children and parents alike. God began to very frequently entrust me with young minds at an incredibly young age. It seemed that babies, children, both young and old came to me with private thoughts and questions that they simply did not feel comfortable talking about with others. I call these moments the "tell me your business" moments. Without even trying, I began to notice that children and parents and some strangers felt comfortable enough to share their dilemmas and challenges with me. In their sharing, I felt a sense of peace, grace, and release as I now absolutely know that it was the hand of God on my life moving me into my purpose.

Note to Self: Oh Lord the journey you have started me on was so strategic and directive. You are simply amazing! Jeremiah 11: 33 He knows the plans for my life (in FULL EFFECT).

I was indeed different from most children. Surely, I could not imagine that this difference was good. In fact, I was told by many that I was strange, a cry baby, skinny and in other words just not cute. You could only imagine how words can just hurt so deeply. Nevertheless, God has and continues to have a plan for my life. As a 51 y/o woman, I now recognize that the enemy started exceedingly early to tear away from me, God's truth, about me. Well, I cannot boast but I will say what my Father in heaven says that I am:

- I am a child of the Most High God.
- I am the head and not the tail,
- I am the lender and not the borrower
- I am above and not beneath,
- I am the righteousness of God
- I have the mind of Christ; therefore, I am a genius,

- I can do all things through my big brother Jesus,
- I am more than a Conqueror,
- NOTHING can separate me from the love of God

to name just a few… As an African American little girl growing up in Spanish Harlem, our neighborhood consisted of Blacks like me, but primarily it was Puerto Ricans, Columbians, Dominicans, and some Cubans. My single mom had to build and create a village for me. My village included other matriarchs who also had southern roots, as some were from NC and SC. My humble beginnings and learning about community started in my home-grown village. This new family like many of my neighbors consisted of many wo were transplants from the south (Charleston, SC) to the north (NYC), as they sought out for better opportunities and search for career advancement. I lived on the corner of 451 West 166 St # 3C, across the street from Rena Daycare Center and adjacent to Edgecombe Park, from which you can see Yankee Stadium located in the Bronx. As I grew up, I later learned to greatly appreciate the rich culture that I was immersed into. I lived down the street from the Audubon Ballroom, formerly known to be filled with Harlem's finest musicians.

It was also known as the place that witnessed Malcom X taking his last breath, as he was assassinated for having a changed mindset. My former home was also known as "Up on the Hill." Today, my place of birth has grown and been renovated and also includes the renown Columbia Presbyterian Hospital, which is known to be a teaching hospital for rising hospital staff. I am so fortunate that God chose little ole me to start here, only to show His glory upon my life.

NOTE to Self: I do not know why I do not speak fluent Spanish, instead I speak Spanglish. Indeed, I am honored to have been brought up alongside such a loving, sweet, and compassionate culture of people who adopted this little Black genius into their homes and hearts. So, I consider myself to be a Woman of God composed by the Author and Finisher of my Fate. I was raised by my African American mother with roots from Charleston SC and adopted into the Puerto Rican family of Jose and Irma Ramirez. This most definitely makes me unique and loved.

TRUST +TRUST +TRUST (x 3) = The Holy Trinity

God the Father, Son and Holy Spirit

My life has and continues to show the wonders of God. I have learned that MY PURPOSE is HIS PLAN and follows HIS PROCESS. HIS PROCESS is just what God allows. We must learn to endure by holding on to what God has said to us, which is usually confirmed in His Word. We are purposed to overcome if and when, we speak daily His word, out loud back to Him. It is good to ask, "Why did this happen to me?" The answer back is "Why not you?" God wants you and me to know that He will use our lives to give him Glory. What better way to give God glory than by allowing your testing to be put on display, so that others may see that you only made it, by His grace. You know "If God be on my side then who can be against me." So, after you have acknowledged the fact that you were chosen by GOD, then know that your living, your pain, your tears, your hurts, and your rejection were not in vain. God uses every single thing in your life for your good. NOTHING is wasted. "Nothing, NO THING!!" You may not see it now, but it will all work out for your good. So, wake up! Shake it off! Now let us regroup and move forward so that your recovery process can begin. Receive it, be healed, and made whole in Jesus' name. **(Note to YOU/the reader: This may take some time.)** Lastly, BE RESTORED. That means get back to work for the Master has need of you. This thing that came to kill, did not kill you but instead it freed you, gave you godly wisdom, better discernment, and of course a CLOSER WALK with GOD.

Now be really honest with yourself, Shhh! nobody but God can hear you. Wasn't it worth it all and to find out that the true prize you received was GOD Himself? If He told us about it, we would pass out and say no way. Instead, if we chose to walk with Him daily; checking on the plan and purpose for our lives, we will be better equipped to handle those life altering events since we GOT God the Father, God the Son and God the Holy Spirit. I could not think of better protectors.

Note to readers: I used the word GOT in the above statement instead of the word HAVE, so that you can understand that at times I may not honor proper word agreement. My purpose is for you to understand that I GOT to Have HIM. No other way to say it. I need Him and I do not care who does not think that it does not sound correct!

Chapter 2:

So, What Does It Mean To Trust?

Trust is defined by Webster's dictionary as a firm belief in the reliability, truth, ability, or strength of someone or something. Belief that someone or something is reliable, good, honest, effective, sincere and will not deliberately do anything to harm you.

Trusting has been so difficult to do. Just like you, I want to control as much as I can (all by myself). WRONG!!!! Tell yourself you do not have the ability to control anything (NOT ONE THING). Even though you think you do. Trust, I mean real Trust, not the kind of trust that is spoken out of comfortability but the kind of trust that transcends your own mind and abilities. Yes, do you or can you TRUST? Everyone's journey leads them to trust God.

You are probably saying "She just doesn't know what I have been through!" "No, I don't trust." but on the inside, be honest with yourself, you really want to. I know how you feel, I've been there too, maybe we are not in the same storm, but my journey and your journey if you acknowledge it, has and will lead you to The Father, my big brother Jesus (the Son) and to my friend, my confidant (The Holy Ghost). All roads lead to God.

Well, the road started before you were in your mother's womb. Honestly, God is the one who selected us to be born in the year we were born, to our parents, our siblings and in our family. He is so specific and so strategic. All He did with you and me was on purpose (kind of cool if you think about it). With His thoughts, He filled us up with His gifts, and gave us an internal desire to love and welcome Him back into the spot that needs and can only be filled by Him for HIM. Like Wow! Awesome! He did all of that to get glory out of our lives. Isn't it a wonderful thing that God thought about me like that! Yes, oh how God loves us. Yes, God loves YOU and me too.

Before you can really know who, you are, you have got to acknowledge where you come from. We come from God. God is love. The world does everything to blind our eyes to God's truth. His love was in my life even when I did not know it or feel it. So, if I go back to my earliest God Collison, where I was in Gods' presence, I was about 5 years old, living in my childhood apartment. I very vividly continue to see now what I saw back then as if it just happened. I remember needing to go to the bathroom in the middle of the night and asking my mother to go with me because I was scared of the dark. I recall being afraid that I would run into a mouse and that I could not stand. My mother would normally get up with me so that I would not be afraid, but this time she vehemently refused and made me be a big girl and go to the bathroom by myself. I remember peeling the covers away slowly as I slipped out from under the warmth of the covers, my feet hit the floor. I felt fear hit me hard. I had to gather the courage to make it to the bathroom without any delays. Regardless of the hesitation in my mind, I repeated "I can do it, you are a big girl." yeah right, instead I should have screamed "I am scared!" The intensity of my full bladder compelled this "Scared dee Cat" to continue into the living room. I stopped immediately. I was so still, that I could not move. I saw in my living room a large male lion with the fullness of his mane laying down with his head erect. It was Majestic in His glory. Both eyes were on me. Did I say the lion was looking at me! My mind ran a mile a second. "If I scream will my mother come, will she believe me, will it eat me. No one will ever believe what I am seeing." I heard my mother yell, "Candy, go to the bathroom right now!" I replied, "Okay Mommy!" I moved slowly still starring back into the eyes of this massive lion that was laying down in my living room. I told myself, "You must be crazy or going crazy."

I ran to the bathroom and finished by business. Fear gripped me as I ran back to the living room and stopped immediately again. I am not crazy, it was still in the same spot, with its eyes fixed on me. As I moved, its head moved ever so slightly to match each step that I took, which let me know that this was no dream. The lion was in a resting position. That scared the heck out of me and for years I never shared that experience with others until I learned that I had a gift to see what others could not see. The mention of this encounter has made aware of who I am.

At the time of this God Collison, God was revealing himself to me, I just did not have any teaching that would have taught me that God talks to His children in so many ways. As a young child and even as an adult, I did not think anyone would believe me if I shared about my lion encounter. I have now found out that my trusting God started back then and has helped me to this day. My Lion of Judah encounter was to tell me as a little girl, I have got you protected and that in the midnight hour, I am always with you. I am here when you are in fear. Let me help you walk in Faith instead of in fear. The Lion of Judah was my beginning of knowing that I was uniquely made. He would choose to show me things that only Candace would understand and that sometimes those things are not meant to be shared. Instead I am to just trust, knowing that it is, **He who is with me.**

You may be saying what does that imaginative story about a Lion and 5-year-old little girl have to do with me and Trust? Well it was my start of recognizing that my prophetic gift showed up early. The lion in my living room was a peak into the spirit realm that back then, I was clueless about. God was letting me know that He was always with me. He showed me in such a powerful way that He was my protector and He was concerned about what concerned me (being afraid of the dark).

God desires for us to rest assured that we shall not walk in fear. So, every night for such a long time I ran to the bathroom looking for the mighty strong lion of which I never saw again. The Lion of Judah has since then shown up in my life in so many ways, that I could keep talking about them until the end of time. His awesome presence has given me peace when I could not find any. His listening ear responds back with a gentle internal gut reply. His unnerving weight causes me to wait for my assignment and not move on until the assignment is complete. My ever growing and God changing relationship with God has made me aware of His goodness for my life. Like so many of you, I unexpectantly came across a tangle God with the introduction of visions and dreams.

God simply talks to me best in my dreams and strong impressions of other's heartfelt emotions and inner thoughts as though they were my very own feelings or thoughts. My ability to dream, is so descriptive and detailed. My dreams seem to be a movie playing out in my sleep. These dreams are often reflective of the future and more than not, come to pass at least minimally in a symbolic way. The gift of dreams should also be accompanied by the gift of interpretation. Some unfortunately do not understand that dreams and vision come from God alone. Instead they use this gift for selfish gain and use the dreams to forecast events without seeking God for His plan and purpose. This gift should in no way be used to gain financial increase but should be used to further the Kingdom of God by speaking life over those who need hope. It is to be used to warn or correct a believer who is walking in disobedience. It is to be used to provide guidance to one who is seeking godly wisdom to reach a specific goal or make a decision. When God chooses to reveal important information through a dream or a vision, I no longer am scared about what I see.   Instead, I have learned to turn the information into a prayer. God will always prepare you. So, if or when He chooses to share about a funeral, I have found that now to be an opportunity to share the gospel in a life-giving way instead of dreading the future because of the loss of a loved one. When you are a believer, death is not a terrible end but instead it should be viewed as a new beginning with Christ Himself. Wow! How glorious that is. The world instead wants us to be overwhelmed about the loss, but I choose to say, that loved one has graduated to heaven and they are now in my future. Being in my future just plainly means I will see them again at the largest family reunion created in glory, Heaven.

We have not because we ask not. Guess what, Candace has learned to ask about everything in prayer. I have emphatically learned that "Prayer changes everything and everything is changed by prayer." I pray about the smallest of concerns to the largest of tragedies, such as a world revival to my son's request to take Physics, just because he wants to and does not have to. I have found that

God is in the details. To some, the smallest little nothing may not be thought of, whereas others may consider a concern to be one of the largest and monumental events of their lives. So, I have learned to have confidence in God and the power of His Might. Let us TRUST God. Believe me He knows what He is doing and is always working it out for our good. He is a good Father. Proverbs 46:10 says, "Be still and know that I am God." Through life's journey, I have found that every situation, circumstance, and human exchange will lead me to several encounters that cause me to Trust God even more.

Chapter 3:

Open My Eyes So That I May See

I want to see what God sees, loves what God loves and hate what God hates. Apart from seeing what God sees, we have to be willing to see the truth, acknowledge the truth and receive the truth and walk in it. "It's one thing to say that you trust God and it is another to actually Trust God. When we walk out on faith it requires that we do so with a constant action of trusting Him in our daily lives." Can you imagine a believer who does not believe or a Christian who does not trust God? I call that "Hypocrisy!" No way that the two go together. I want to be a Christian who shows that I trust God by my actions of love and obedience. To love God means to be obedient to His word. You must have both!!!!

Trust in His character,

Trust in His Word,

Trust in His Love,

Trust Him when you cannot see Him.

God sees the Jesus in us and on our lives and He sees the enemy who uses unaware people to counter His plan and purpose. Open my eyes that I may see.

There are no coincidences in God. He sees and knows all. God's molding of our lives is so tender, so specific, and so indeed loving. If you believe then you will trust in the God that we serve. Yes, God is good! Even when we do not know or feel His goodness, He is in the midst of our darkest hours. He covers us and carries us to a new season. This is where trust begins. It is here where God carries us when we are too weak to walk or even talk or pray. Look back and see where He carried you by sending you a kind word from a friend, when you received an unexpected check in the mail, when someone took your kids away for the weekend, when you got a good report from the doctors' office. See it, this where and when God picked you up in His loving arms and gave you the rest that you so needed.

The Bible says 2 Kings 6:13-17 explains "Go, find out where he is, the king ordered, so I can send men and capture him." The report came back: "He is in Dothan." Then he sent horses and chariots and a strong force there. They went by night and surrounded the city. When the servant of the man of God got up and went out early the next morning, an army with horses and chariots had surrounded the city. "Oh, my lord, what shall we do?" the servant asked. "Don't be afraid," the prophet answered. "Those who are with us are more than those who are with them and Elisha prayed, "O LORD, open his eyes so he may see." Then the Lord opened the servant's eyes, and he looked and saw the hills full of horses and chariots of fire all around Elisha.

Chariots were powerful military vehicles. Warriors in the chariots, drawn by horses trained for battle, had surrounded the entire city of Dothan. So as Elisha and his servant walked around the wall, they saw a military force aligned against them at every point. There was no escape. But Elisha said to his servant, "We've got them just where we want them now. There are more of us than of them." Can you imagine, the servant must have looked at him as if he had lost his mind. Dothan was a small walled city. It was in a valley ringed by mountains on which the servant of Elisha saw the chariot and horses of fire. God's provision and power had been there all along, but the servant had not been able to see it. Remember, Elisha's own crisis of faith had concerned whether he would see the chariot and horses of fire when they came for Elijah. Already he had faced the issue, "Will I trust God, see the invisible, and believe in the strength and authority of heaven even when it cannot be measured with my physical senses?" In like manner he prayed for his servant to apprehend truth that required faith to see. It is a marvelous privilege to be able to pray for a struggling friend, for the believing heart next to us that is fearful and beaten down. "I've tried to tell them as much as I can, but, O Lord, you have to make it real."

Note: Sometimes the best way to share your faith is to show your FAITH in Action!!

How many us know that **A Crisis will Grow Your Faith** and Elisha's crisis had concerned whether he would have his eyes opened to see how God acted and where God was present. Would he be able to declare invisible realities that others could not see-chariots and horses of fire, the wonders and power of God? Would he be able to speak confidently not just about how the world appeared but also about the ways of God? He had and we have lots of uncertainties, BUT GOD.

Tell yourself (Out Loud) "But God!!" We soon see what Elisha had faith to see. Trusting God shows up when there is no more that we can possibly do. The Invisible God makes all things possible. Elisha responded to his servant's fear by simply saying "Fear not, for those with us are more than those with them." (2 Kings 6:16) Elisha then prayed "Lord, I pray you, open his eyes that he may see, and the Lord opened the young man's eyes, and he saw and behold the mountain was full of horses and chariots of fire round about Elisha. (2 Kings 6:17)

Each of us experiences this world through our five senses–touch, taste, smell, hearing and seeing. It is how God created us. But he did not stop there. He also created us with spiritual eyes and spiritual ears, to see and hear things that are spiritually discerned. It should be our personal desire to fight spiritual blindness by simply opening our hearts and mouths towards heaven. "Prayers of the righteous availeth much." The prophet Elisha in the passage twice prayed very simply, "Open their eyes." He prayed for insight, perception and the recognition of glorious things that were otherwise hidden.

Trusting in God means to know that He knows what is best for us, not we ourselves. When we realize that God is simply in control, then it is so freeing to know that all things will work out for our good, no matter what we see or hear physically. You may not understand or be able to see your way out, but it is you who allows for His truth, His peace, and His grace to always surround you with His love.

Trusting God usually is mirrored in the flawless love, which is often evident in our close relationships. Unfortunately, the mirror that we look into for others is flawed because people truly do not have the ability to love unconditionally and be trusted, as a result of Adam's sinful nature. We are to learn from other loving relationships, and they ought to mirror godliness. Do not get stuck when they cannot and will not. When we look at close relationships, we must be practical and understand that no one person on this earth will be able to complete you like Jesus can and will. Your mom, dad, your spouse and even your children will do their best to love you in a God kind of way, but they are not truly capable to love you the way that God can. God's love endures all things. His love covers a multitude of sins. He is so faithful, even we are not faithful. Be mindful that all things are possible with God. He must be a part of your daily equation.

GOD + ME = Trusting GOD

It has been my experience that I learned to trust my family and only them. I have since then, learned that I have shifted in that thought process. I now Trust whole heartedly completely and totally put my trust in the Lord. I Trust God!! For me to make such a bold statement, I have had many encounters in life where He has been glorified. My good and close friends and family members at some point have caused me to doubt their love or commitment to me and for me, but not God. God has been there for me when no one was or cared to be there. I have experienced close family and friends walking away when things seemed to be too much. I can testify that my God has never left or forsaken me. He has been a constant help in times of trouble. He has been so good to me, to the point where I have chosen to write to you about our relationship. My journey has proven time and time again that "I WIN" as long as I put Him first in my life. He will always get the glory out of my life. I look for God in everything that I come across; friendships, employment assignments, doctors' appointments, selecting vehicles to building a new home. I have to find Him, or I cannot do it. In other words, I need God to show me that whatever I am doing, I need to know that He is for me and part of all of my decisions.

In my own battle with fear, I often find myself focusing on life through my natural senses, and truly little on my spiritual senses. **Too often, I let what I feel or what I see determine what I believe. But that is backwards. I need to let what I believe determine how I feel and even what I see, spiritually.** Let me explain it this way:

there is a difference between *facts* and *truth*. Facts are what you experience naturally, with your five senses, but truth happens at a deeper level, at a spiritual level. Very often, truth must be seen with spiritual eyes. We must reprogram our thinking to focus on truth so that it can supersede the facts of our situation. When we focus on facts, we focus on the carnal (natural) things of this world. But, when we focus on truth, we focus on the spiritual things of God. There is peace when we are spiritually minded, but there is fear, depression, and anxiety when we are naturally minded. Romans 8:6 makes this clear: "For to be carnally minded is death, but to be spiritually minded is life and peace." If you want life and peace, then you must become spiritually mind- ed.

Chapter 4:

The Pit Is Necessary

You may have said, "I want to trust you, God, But I don't know how to." The people that I have trusted have hurt me, harmed me, pushed me down, talked about me, ignored me, rejected me, stolen my innocence, lied to me, deceived me, molested me, manipulated me, cheated on me, slapped me, were two faced, belittled me, loud talked me, gossiped about me, persecuted me." All of these sufferings caused me to run away from the fear of being hurt again. I ran away from the torment and terror that plagued my mind and yet again being mistreated by those in whom I trusted. I cried out to God saying that "I have too many tears to count, so many sleepless nights and stomach aches that have caused by soul to ache."

It has been said that our tears are collected so that all we go through in life is never in vain. You mean "my pain is not in vain?" and that "MY PAIN HAS PURPOSE?" We often times can relate our pain to being placed in a pit.

Psalms 40:1 - 2 says *"I waited patiently for the lord; and He inclined to me and heard my cry. He also brought me up out of a horrible pit, out of the miry clay, and set my feet upon a rock, and established my steps."*

A place or situation of futility (what is the point?), a place of misery or degradation, your pit may even be like a prison, a state of confinement or captivity- in other words a place of pure hell on earth. You know, the brick wall. The place in your life when you will need the power of the living God to get your through a seemingly hopeless circumstance or situation.

Everybody in this life will experience pit experiences. Your Pit experience maybe the pain felt from a bully at school, a difficult subject that seems overwhelming or maybe for you adults your pit experience may have come from rejection, a loss of a job, a shaken marriage, or even handling a difficult child. You see trials no doubt will come. But when they come, "How do you handle them?" Are you complacent? Do you worry? Or do you just complain? Whatever your methods have been in the past, today is the day that you should try something new. You see God wants you utterly understand how you can get through your pit experience. Whatever your pit is, you need to know that there is a way to wait on your promise. You see the pit is necessary as a part of the process to elevate you into God's purpose according to His intended plan. Since God is the Alpha and the Omega, he sees the beginning to the end and astoundingly He will give you a glimpse of your future without revealing the before, the during, and the final steps of your process. Now as a blood brought believer, it important for you to know what God's purpose and intent is for your life. Though we may feel unsure, scared, and uncertain. It is imperative to remember and hold on to God's spoken promise. You see the seed has already entered into your heart and your faith allows it to grow and grow. The growth of the hidden seed begins in a pit, it begins in a place of darkness. The pit is indeed necessary. The pit has now become the darkened incubator for a miracle. I know you say well, I do not want to be in this darkened place, it is tight, it is confined, it is restrictive, and I am all alone. But that is the best place to get the birth of the seed to come forth. The seeds' place on the inside of each and every one of us, is God's purpose for our lives in the earth. The Pit is necessary. If you could just imagine in the natural how a real seed grows it sits in a pit & when it sits and is positioned by the creator for His intended purpose it begins to grow. You see the incubator of most miracles begin with humble beginnings. The Pit along with water allows the maturation process to begin. The process, yes, the process though not liked or even welcomed by most Christians is necessary to get to an expected end.

The Pit is Necessary. The creator will allow certain unpleasant circumstances to begin our humbling process. It is necessary for us all to walk in a humbled state. **James 4:6 says the Lord resist the proud but gives grace to the humble.**

The Pit is Necessary for purging, it is necessary for getting rid of unwanted waste. You know the place to get rid of the spirit of doubt the place to get rid of your isms and schisms, a place to get rid of what ifs. All of that nastiness & foolishness has just Got to go. They all must be purged out of your spirit. Got to go.

The Pit is Necessary, because it is a place that is a confined space and restricts any movement except for upward. Yes, upward bound, should be your thought process. My thoughts should be, "I am too low to go lower. The only way to get up and out is to focus on the Lord in the pit. The focus upward can seem long, and tedious but hard work never hurt anyone. The effort made towards moving upward allows one to build stamina, strength, and endurance. But do not get discouraged, it often times will not come over night. The confined space also restricts the access of others to you. You see true friends will encourage you to never quit & keep it moving. But those who are happy hanging in the dirt will encourage you to let go of your dream and your promise. You know they say things like. You cannot do that. Who do you think you are, no one has ever done that? - The Naysayers.

In your Pit Experience- Cry *out to God* for help. For My God shall supply all of my needs according to His riches in glory. Remember that God is your source and all good things come from the Lord. Your time spent alone will give you time to read the word, to pray the word and to speak the word.

The Pit is Necessary. The process is on God's timeline. You see a day to God is like a thousand years to man. You must have *patience.* So, patience is not just something to hope for or even think about, Patience is the only way to wait on the Lord. The word "patiently" means without tiring and with perseverance. To come out of the pit takes time and requires patience. Trouble does not last always. There is purpose in the pit. The pit is a time of preparation, a time of rest and a time for healing.

We must remember to look to hills from which my help comes. All my help comes from the Lord. Count on God to come through with what He has promised. He is well able to perform it. God loves us through the process. The pit is necessary for all of us to go through in order for God to get the maximum output from our lives. In other words, **"God will get the glory."** There is triumphant victory that comes out of the pit, there is wisdom that comes from the pit. There is a now a more mature Woman of God, now a stronger Man of God that has been transformed into a beautiful creation pressed forth out of darkness into the marvelous light.

Breakthrough is at Hand

Once God says that it is time, there is nothing holding you back from your breakthrough. The Pit is a place of preparation. It is a place where your character is changed, groomed, and developed. Your pit situation is meant to show you and others truly what you are made of. Sometimes we really do not know what is on the inside of us until it is tested. God has made us to be more than conquerors. That means that we have conquered some challenges in our lives, some pits, and we have overcome them by the power of God, not in our own strength but by the POWER OF GOD. Bishop Morton sings the song "I'm still standing, I'm still holding on to what I believe. I 'm motivated fully persuaded, I'm still standing on the word that's in my heart." Which means that is what we are meant to do when all is said and done to just STAND. Stand with God. Stand firm in His promises. Stand on His Word. Like Elder Johnson says with our youth, "Put the word on it." Just do not quit, do not give up for God is still at work.

Just remember that we are to trust in God, just like in **Job 13:15a says** *"though He slay me yet will I trust him. I will trust him."*

and **Philippians 1:6:** *I am sure that God who began the good work within you will keep on helping you to grow in his grace until within you is finally on that day when Jesus Christ returns.* Thank God that He is not done with us yet. He is preparing us for himself as a bride is in waiting to receive her bridegroom. We must stand at the ready, in wait for our Savior's second coming. Waiting is not passive. **So, Get Ready, Be Ready and Stay Ready!** Stay encouraged that God is yet working miracles even in the pits of our lives. **LOOK AT THE BIG OAK TREE BELOW-** The seed cannot become an oak tree without the process.

You say if God is good and I believe in Him then why do I feel so much pain? Good question and the answers are found in trusting God. Trusting His purpose, His plan, for He knows to plan for your life. Jeremiah 29:11. "Yes, I too have been denied, told you are no good. BUT I speak to every lie, to every demon from hell assigned to my life and I say I am a child of the Most High God and Kingship resides in my spirit." So, I open my mouth wide and loud and I proclaim the word of God in the atmosphere, I say I change my atmosphere, my family, my friends, my life, with the words that come out of my mouth, do you understand the words that are coming out of my mouth?" LOL

I SPEAK LIFE over everything that I encounter that does not line up with the word of God. I command all crooked things to be made straight. I declare the change that I want to see. I speak it over and over until I see the manifested change, until I can give my praise report. Trust is all that I know to do especially in the middle of betrayal, lies, in the face of those who have turned their backs on me, and those who I thought would always be there. I speak to the impossible. I speak to the unbelievable. I say move out of my way mountain, MOVE in the name of Jesus Christ. I declare and decree life over my life and all those connected to me, I speak it, I believe it and I decree it and I say Amen, knowing that it is so. Then I wait in faith to receive what I have spoken until my prayer manifests back in a tangible response from God.

When God speaks a word to you, TRUST Him to know that it will come to pass. No matter how long ago He said it, it will happen. It will happen. It will happen. It will happen for His thoughts are higher than mine. He knows what is best for my life. He is the Author and the Finisher of my Faith and that which He started He will finish it. In other words, all things will work out for my good. Yes, even the bad things that have happened to me will be changed in such a magnificent way what His glory will transform the evil into good. Please remember that God knows what He is doing and if I honestly say that I am His then I am to follow Him daily by trusting Him daily.

2 Timothy1:9 says *Who has saved us and called us with a holy calling, not according to our works, but according to His own purpose and grace which was given to us in Christ Jesus before world began.*

Ephesians 1:11 NIV *In Him we were also chosen, having been predestined according to the plan of him who works out everything inconformity with the purpose of His will.*

Do You Know Your Purpose?

You Must Not Know About Me, "I am a Child of the King."

Webster's dictionary defines the word purpose - something set up as an object or end to be attained : INTENTION *b* : RESOLUTION, DETERMINATION , as a subject under discussion or an action in course of execution or to propose as an aim to oneself.

Webster also defines conformity as: action in accordance with some specified standard or authority.

Let us look at it from God's perspective because Webster cannot tell me how to be me, only God knows all about my purpose. So, you say God, "What is my purpose, because I'm not quite sure?"

Remember that there is a process to the purpose to release God's Promises

**PROCESS ----------PURPOSE----------
PROMISES**

Steps to Finding Your Purpose and Your Identity in Christ:

1. You must know who you are and whose you are.
2. Your purpose must be made known to you at any early age or you will fall to deception,

lies, and mischief through your on and off walk with God- Stay on the path. The enemy will lure you from the things of God if you do not know who you are.

3. He will use peer pressure to do ungodly things like trying sex, drugs, alcohol just to fit in, distractions like Facebook and Twitter, ungodly soul ties will coerce you not to fulfill the will of God in our life.

4. To know your Purpose, the only one who is able to truly tell you who you are is God, but if you are not seeking his face, if you are not reading his word, if you are not asking Jesus to save your soul, then you cannot hear God tell you about how much he loves you and how He has a perfect plan for your life. Jeremiah says, "I know the plans I have for you to prosper you and not to harm you."

5. Do not doubt your identity and purpose in Christ. We are to be kingdom minded. You must learn early to discern good from evil. You must be able to know for yourself who your haters are and who your helpers are. God has placed many wonderful people in our lives like: our parents, grandparents, our aunts, uncles, our Pastor, teachers, even your neighbors to help you get to where you got to get to in CHRIST. You must also recognize the haters that are also assigned by the devil to get you off your path, to get you to be confused and to be misguided.

How do you Recognize Helpers and Haters?

- Helpers will protect, guide, and lead you to God.
- Haters will lie to you and give you the big head about yourself.
- Helpers will tell you to stay humble and meek just like Jesus.
- Haters will lure you into places of sin, they will put you down, they will attempt to control you, and make you feel guilty for thinking differently from the norm.
- Helpers will encourage you when you are down. They will make you smile. They will tell you God's truth. They will help you to get to your future as they are lifelong cheerleaders cheering you onto your destiny. Helpers teach us to be respectful, to be kind and to have compassion for others.

Thank God for both, because we need the helpers to do God's will, but we also need the Hater to keep us on our knees praying for God's purpose, protection, and wisdom. Remember that "all things work together for our good for those who are called according to His purpose." Knowing your purpose should help you seek God's wisdom, to seek God's knowledge and God's understanding.

Wisdom helps us in so many ways. It will help you avoid great tragedies happening in our lives. If we would just seek God's choices in our decisions. The renewing of our minds with the word of God will help you not to walk in disobedience, to not walk in rebellion and not have bad attitudes. God purpose for your life is to make a difference in the world. Everything you do both big and small matters to God. Whatever bothers you bothers God. So, because He is concerned about us, why can't we just ask God to help us with everything? Do not just talk to him sometimes but talk to Him every day. Ask God, what do you want me to do? Instead of always asking God to do something for us.

Let us get back to the PROCESS, which leads us to His PURPOSE and provides all God's PROMISES.

Tell the Story of Samuel choosing David to be the next King of Israel-

Finding David- the last Son of Jessie- does not look like a king on the outside.

Daily routine of being a great shepherd- took his job seriously

Protected the sheep from a bear and a lion

THE PROCESS IS NECESSARY- God is preparing you now for greater works for His glory.

David was purposed by God to defeat Goliath, but he wouldn't have been able to walk in confidence to do so, if he had not spent lots of time with God, talking, praying and forming a relationship with God in the fields as a shepherd.

As he spent time with God, God changed his focus and strengthened him to defend the sheep and defeat the enemies' attack- (lions and bears).

Slaying Goliath was one of David's purposes, but he took no credit for himself, he did it to magnify his Father in heaven.

Later God prepared David to become a great king, who chased after God's heart. Read the book of Psalms as David shows us how he admonished God and asks for God's help quite often.

God has prepared places for us to go when we know and find our purpose in Him.

Some Things to Remember:

- Turn away from people, places and things that will not lead you to God.
- Be strong, do not quit or doubt who you are and whose you are.
- Ask God to give you His wisdom. Scripture says, "as a man thinketh, so is he." So be who God says you are. – You are the head and not the tail. You are above and not beneath. You are the lender and not the

borrower. You are the righteousness of God. I can do all things through God who strengthens me.

- See yourself that way God sees you.
- Change your focus. Find your passion. Set your eyes on the things of God.
- Have a good attitude. Smile, laugh and have fun.
- Do not be a know it all, instead be a learn it all.
- Know that God loves you and that he has a perfect plan for your life. Let Him lead you. Your Purpose is to Find God and remember that it is not about us, but it is about Jesus.

When God speaks a word to you, trust Him to know that it will come to pass. No matter how long ago He said it. It will happen. It will happen. It will happen.

Our Father is a Good Father. Just like the song says "that's who He is, and I am loved by Him, that's who I am." He is perfect in all of His ways. Trust is built on knowing that it could not have been any other than God to have raised me by a single mom. I did not have a Daddy, but I now have a good Father. It is not easy but one thing that I can rest on knowing, is that the way to move forward from tragedy is to do the hard things and to forgive the unforgiveable. Honestly, Jesus said it best "forgive them for they know not what they do." So, if Jesus did it, then yes beloved you must forgive as well. This hard thing is the key in moving into a place of peace. Release them and do as Jesus did give it all to God and forgive out of love for Jesus. You will never feel like forgiving or may never want to, but it is still required that you release yourself to your peace. Forgive, Jesus did. Press the play button and let us make God smile. He says "Yes, that is my beloved daughter or son." When you are weak, He is strong. Allow God's strength to quicken your spirit to move forward and walk in your purpose.

Chapter 5: My Father's Dream

I remember a dream that I had that showed me just how much God loved me. In the dream I was about 5 years old and not the woman that I am today. I remember feeling so tired, overwhelmed, hurt, and scared all at the same time. I felt bewildered and just could not do anything at all. It seemed like all that I tried on my own made no progress but instead zapped me of all my mental, spiritual, and physical energy. As I gazed ahead, I found myself to be in dessert land with no trees, no water, no shade, and no people. I was most definitely alone. I knew on the inside that the dessert was the place I needed to go through to get to my destination. As I contemplated, my inability to take a step forward, a gray-haired older man appeared out of nowhere. He was standing by my side. I looked up at him and without saying anything, he began to speak, and he said, "God did not give." I finished the scripture out loud and I said, "Me the spirit of fear but of love, power and of a sound mind." Those words spoken reminded me of who I was and that I was not alone. My help was with me in times of trouble.

The Bible says that He will hide me. Well, God did one better He carried me. Without me asking He said He would take me. I instantly thought how wonderful He was to take me at least part of the way and then I may be able to make the rest of the way. So, this kind gray haired man picked this little girl up in His strong comforting arms. I felt so safe, I felt His strength instantly. I felt His love and devotion for me as I nestled up in His arms. My heartbeat felt His heartbeat. The sound of His heart beating and the movement of His bounce as He walked with me in His arms felt so good that I quickly fell asleep. I finally was able to rest, when days and weeks before, I had not slept because of all the problems that showed up at my doorstep.

The way ahead seemed so far away and when I awoke, I looked out from His shoulder and found that we had arrived. He let me down so gently and stood me up on my two feet. I remember feeling revived, rested and so much stronger now. I didn't have enough "Thank You's" in my mouth to tell him how much I appreciated His caring for me, His loving me, His carrying me, His protecting me, and His showing up right on time. I realized that the older gray-haired man was God. He showed me with such a beautiful illustration in this dream, how much He loves me and that He promises never to leave or forsake me. He is a very present help in time of trouble. I could not help thinking about how He carried me ALL the way, not part of the way BUT ALL THE WAY! I asked, "Who does that?" He softly answered, "God does that." I am so thankful to such a wonderful Father who cares about what I care about, so much that He sent His only son, Jesus to take my place. It should have been me on the cross. What a Wonderful Savior! What a Mighty God we serve!

Chapter 6:

My Testimony. They Harmed Me But You Healed Me

DREAM IN THE DARKNESS

The dream that I shared with you came at one of the lowest and most devastating times in my life. I dreamed that I was sucked into a black abyss of never-ending darkness. I remember falling down into a cave. All I could see was complete darkness that I had fallen and somehow, I managed to catch and hold onto a long rope that was centered in the middle of the dark cavern. For a moment I felt lost, and helpless as I looked upward and below me and saw nothing. I could not tell how far up I was or how far down I was. It was just dark. As I hung there, holding on for my life, I instantly remembered who I was. When I remembered who I was, I yelled out, "JESUS!" Every time I called out "JESUS!" I gained the strength to pull myself up this rope. As I cried out to God and called the name that is above every name, I began to rise up and above my circumstance. I kept calling "Jesus! Jesus!" Each time I cried out "Jesus", I climbed higher up the rope and the darkness became less, as light flooded the cavern. I could now see upward, and I felt that I could make it, but not on my own. I would only make it with God. I gained strength in Christ and I was able to climb up and up. By this time, I could see people on the edge of the cavern. I wondered, why weren't they helping me? Why didn't they come when I called for help? Why were they just watching and not helping me get to safety? Their glares made me more determined to climb with Jesus. I kept calling and He kept strengthening me until I was able to swing the rope to a ledge and climb up and through a white open window that was within my reach.

God revealed to me that this dream showed that I could have died but I found strength in Christ. That I should not and could not do it in my own strength. God showed me that others would watch for my demise, for my fall and that some would watch in awe of what God was doing in my life. They would see how God came to help me come up and out of this darkness. God said that no one could help me other than the name of Jesus. Jesus is the answer for all and to all things that we encounter. Breakthrough is ahead if you faint not. I had to keep my eyes upward and not look beneath me because I would lose my focus on Christ. He promised that He would never leave or forsake me. He told me that He loved me and that I did not do anything wrong. I was chosen to show others how He would make it right in my life. No doubt!! That is just what he did. Jesus did it!!!

Someone made a call to The Department of Social Services (DSS) and my three children were removed from my home for two months.

I was called in my program manager's office and she explained that they received a child welfare anonymous call reporting abuse in my home. As a result of the false report, my three children were temporarily removed from my home and placed in a church member's home as kinship care. My children were to have no contact with their father during the investigation. During this time, I was in the battle of my life. I had to position myself in a place that I had to encourage my children, my husband and at the end of the day come home to an empty house and encourage myself. My husband stayed in a furnished apartment, I lived at our family's home alone with Zoey (our dog) and my babies (my three children) stayed with what I thought was a family friend.

Through it all, we never stopped paying our tithes and continued to give offerings. I cannot explain all that God did for us during this time, but financially we had all we needed and even wanted during this time. My children's grades never slipped. They got A's and B's like they always had. I do not know how but I went to work every day. I felt helpless and somewhat lost. Every day I spoke to myself because I had to be strong for everyone else.

I remember the first night that I was alone. The house was quiet from the sound of missing children. I cried out to God. I screamed at my pain. I cried, I wept, I cried, and I wept some more until I cried myself to sleep. Then I felt like someone was in the room with me. I felt like someone was standing over me. Without opening my eyes, I felt His strength and His comfort and protection. He bent down to my ear and said, "Unsubstantiated!" As I wondered what I heard, He said it again "Unsubstantiated!" I then opened my eyes and said out loud what I heard. I said "Unsubstantiated!" God thank you for answering me. Thank you for loving me. Thank you coming to me. So, I got up with the joy on the inside that what God said I would have to carry His word in my heart and stand on it until it came to pass. I felt weary and it did not look like it would shift in my favor, but I learned that God is forever faithful. No matter what this world shows you, it does not matter;

nevertheless, what does matter is only what God says.

My family was separated from me for 2 months. It felt like an eternity. I learned the names of the devils that came against me and we went to war. I was in the fight of my life, the fight for my sanity, for my children and for my husband. I stood on the God's shoulders. The enemy showed up in many faces. Those that I thought would be with me and for me, left me. How incredibly painful it was to see the masses separate themselves because of this ugly lie. Those who wanted to believe the worst walked away. I began to truly see the hearts of man. Those who have smiled in my face became deceptive in nature, two faced. I could not believe the treachery that I received. All I knew was that I would get through and I also knew it would not be easy. Speak life, speak life, speak life, so I did. When I was tired, when I was frustrated, when I was hurt and overwhelmed; I spoke back what I heard God say to me on the first night. "Unsubstantiated." I truly had to fight for my deliverance. Every day, every month, and every year, I fought to get in the right place with God and stay there.

Who would do such a terrible thing? What pit did they crawl out of? Why? Why Me?

I heard God say why not you? You have all you need on the inside of you to get through this and when it is all said and done you will proclaim my glory to the nonbelievers and encourage the believers that with God All Things are Possible. I chose you and your family to show my favor and glory upon your lives. I wanted to show that I love you even when all things are not good. I will work it all out for your good.

Spirits that I battled during this Storm were:

Rebellion, disobedience, conformity, selfishness, ungodly soul ties, familiar spirits, spirit of lust, homosexuality, lying demons, spirit of manipulation, python spirit, covetous spirit, religious and traditional spirits, occult spirits, spirit of works, spirit of guilt and shame, rejection, exclusion, abandonment, treacherous spirits, and the spirit of divination.

I came against every last one and God gets the victory. He delivered me out of the pit that was meant to kill me and wound my soul. We won Jesus! We won Jesus!! I have grown in the knowledge of the spirit realm. It is real. I faced these demons and the Christ on the inside of me rose up and overcame it all. Jesus said that He overcame the world and because He lives in me, I have that same power and authority to overcome the works of the devil.

God instructed me to pray for those who despitefully used me, to pray for my enemies. To be honest, I did not want to, I clearly wanted God's vengeance on them for my pain. God explained that it was His will not that one soul will perish, so I surrendered my will for His will, and I began to pray out of obedience because I love God. I trust God. So, I to this day continue to pray for those who have intentionally and unintentionally hurt me and my family. It is not easy to bless those who have hurt you, but if I believe and trust God then I will choose to be obedient to God's will and not to my will.

My prayer sounded like this: Lord help, (list the names of those who have hurt you here: ___? ____, ____, etc.) that hurt me. Lord bless those who cursed me. Lord help those who despitefully used me. Lord forgive them for hurting me and my family. Lord bring them to a place of repentance and save their souls. Lord give them an understanding of their actions so that it will not happen to not another person or family. In Jesus name, Amen.

I found that in order to release myself from the sting of this treacherous act, I have to forgive them and release them so that I could move forward. I am still in the process of moving forward. Some days are better than others, but with every new morning I have yet another chance to walk this out with Jesus. I am so glad that I have Jesus. I never want to ever experience a lack of his presence. He is the air that I breathe. I cannot and will not live without Christ in my life. Without Him I am nothing. Without Him I have nothing. With Him I am His and He is mine. One way to move forward is to listen to the Holy Spirit who lives within us.

WHAT IN THE WORLD! Why would she say such an ugly thing, where is this all really coming from?"

This cut me so deep, it was a crushing blow that hit us to the very core of our souls. It deeply wounded us. God this is so wrong! I recall spiraling down into a deep dark hole. A heaviness rose over my heart. Wounded from the inside and afflicted from the outside. My pain was immeasurable. This attack from the enemy caused me to question my faith. Yes, I honestly was in doubt of who I was, but not who God is. Outwardly, this felt so bad, but way down on the inside I heard myself say do not give up and it will be okay. I have to be strong for my family

I was tired. I was weary and I was beaten on the inside. My inner strength was all gone, I do not even know how I got up daily. I was in constant pain, for my heart ached relentlessly for my babies. The thing that I grew up loving and living for was being torn out of my hands. How could this be happening to me? I am the one who babysits and watches children. I am a watchman on the wall for children. I consider myself to be a gate guard. No one will get by me, not on my watch. How did this happen? Who would do such a thing to me? I had all these questions rise up daily in my head. I was fighting an internal battle to keep my sanity. I felt like I was going to lose my mind. I could not even tell my own mother that DSS, the place I worked for helping children to survive and thrive had now knocked on my door and moved my children from my home. Besides my children being moved, my husband was not allowed any contact as well. Just like DSS, there was an investigation to find out if the allegations were factual. The allegations started next door with our neighbor and were echoed by a demonic attack that raised a suspicion of abuse to my neighbor and to my children.

The devil is on his job, so I better be on my Job. For if I allow what he is trying to do then all is lost. So, at the very beginning I spoke out loud God's word. I spoke it because it is all I knew to do. It was my lifeline. I had no choice but to stand on His word and it was my trying period. I felt alone and confused. I wanted to call my mommy and other family members but knew inside that they really could not help me. It was only God that would save me from this. I had to be strong when I felt so weak. I had to speak God's word when the atmosphere tried to kill me. My soul was being attacked by lies, lies, lies. So, I began to speak out of my belly "I TRUST, I TRUST, I TRUST GOD!" I yelled it for the world to hear. I trust you God; I don't care what they say. I trust that you are with me even though I feel alone. I trust that you will never leave me. I trust you God even when those who said that had my back talked about me and walked away. I trust you God. For those who made the call to DSS (with all attempts being made behind closed doors to bring me to my knees by breaking my heart). My heart was shattered into a million pieces as I saw my children daily (by the grace of God). They wanted to go home, they asked about their father and, where was he? As I looked into my children's crying faces asking "Mommy why is this happening to us. What is going to happen, Mommy?" I said as a proclamation, as a declaration. I said it by Faith and to make sure that the devil heard me loud and clear. I said "God is with us and it is well. WE will be reunified, and God will get the glory out of this. You will do well in school and one day we will help someone else who will go through what we have come out of. We will be okay. God promised me!"

DSS put in place that I was not alone with my children and that I had to always be escorted by an approved third party. I was not allowed to take them to school or attend anything at school without a preapproved DSS appointee. I felt helpless but not hopeless. No matter how long it took and the delays that kept popping up, God reassured me from within that we will all be okay. I had to trust the Almighty God that I would tell others about. I learned about the Sovereignty of God in a different way.

I found comfort in His promises and I found comfort in seeing my children's faces every day. I could not sleep where they were staying but I was allowed to come in the mornings before school and after school before they went to bed. As a mother, it made me feel good to still be able to care for them even in the small ways. I would take their clothes home and wash them. I would help them with homework after I got off from work. I would buy clothing and special food items like candy when they asked or it. I wanted to take away the pain of being separated from their parents, but I could not. So, I did all that I knew to do, I prayed with them and encouraged them that God was in control. I told them daily to trust God. Randy and I were able to give their caregiver $200 to $300 weekly in support of this family's increase. While separated as a family and living in three different locations, we still gave our tithes and offerings without delay.

I made my way to church because I was able to see my children there as well. I did not feel like it. I knew that people were whispering about me and my family. I had to block out the external chatter and hear from the one who created me. He said, "Greater is He that is in you than he that is in the world." He said, "you can do all things through Christ who strengthens me." He said we always win. He said raise up your head and show them that I am your father and you are my daughter. As a wife, I had to encourage my heartbroken husband that if God be for us then who can be against. These allegations came straight after my children, my marriage, and my life. If fear had its way, I would lose my children into the DSS foster care system, lose my husband to a prison sentence, and lose my conviction in trusting God as a Woman of God. I had to fight daily for my sanity. I had too much to lose, but if I truly trusted God, I had all to gain. So, I placed my trust in God, no matter what I saw, what was said, who talked about me, who did not understand. I did not care. I would be victorious just like God told me I would. I held onto His promise.

During this process I found out what I was made of. I found out how many people are so phony and fake. This tore me up from the inside out. I found out that lies by those who do not know the Holy Spirit are easy to believe. People tend to believe what they hear and not what they know. I learned of a strength that I did not give myself. I learned of a faithfulness that was enduring. I learned of a love that was endless.

Unfortunately, when you live and profess God, please know that there are people who want to prove that you are not who you say you are. They want to make you out to be a liar, like they are. God did not reveal the treachery while I was going through the valley of the shadow of death. I was merely passing through. People that I would and have given my last to came against me for the sake of doing something for my good. They were and are cowards that are spineless and were being used in a demonic assignment. Please tell me who would find solace in taking a mother away from her children? What God forsaken person or people would be okay with causing my children to suffer like that?

I hurt so much that my soul hurt. I later found out that people who went to my former church and were close to my family made an anonymous call to DSS without establishing the facts. That call forever changed me and my family. We were all hurt to our souls. We are still recovering from the thought of not having one another. My oldest has gone away to college and has a difficult time being away from her family and has many trust issues as a direct result of our family's separation. Somebody say, **BUT GOD......**

Now let me tell you about all the praise reports that came to my family as a result of proving the devil wrong.

- God built us two homes that were prophetically spoken to us 10 years before all of this happened.
- My husband received a promotion and a new position.

- We received a new church family and are delivered from wrong thinking.
- All family members know God without a doubt and regularly go to God on behalf of others as intercessors.
- We were taught to reject the lies spoken about us and pick up the mandate from God to tell a dying world about the Jesus we serve.
- God taught us how to forgive those who hurt us and pray that they come to know and love Him the way we do.
- God allowed us to share our testimony that gives God glory, as my family loves one another unapologetically.
- God released my family from ungodly soul ties.
- God delivered us from the lies of the enemy.
- Gave us God's truth that we are fearfully and wonderfully made in His likeness and image.
- I am proud to belong to God and He belongs to me.
- I know that I know that I know…. That God loves us. There is no wall you won't kick down; lie you won't tear down coming after me (song sung by Cory Asbury called Reckless Love).

- God showed my family who were our friends whether it was for a long or short season.
- God showed us who our foes were and how to declare God's word against each demonic assignment.
- We spoke the word at the beginning and did not stop until the spoken word manifested in our lives.

Chapter 7:

God's Grace is Sufficient

Trust God the Father. He is a loving, Protector, Provider, and Caregiver who comforts His children.

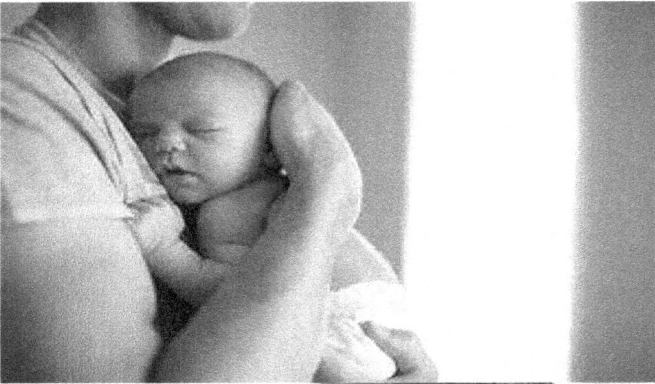

Can you see it? As the Father holds us close to comfort us, feed us, rock us to sleep, He already knows who you are and who you will be. His plan is to prosper us. His hold is so endearing. He is proud that you are His. You are His masterpiece.

Trust, God the Son. You know Him, his name is Jesus Christ. He looks out for you for our Big Daddy in Heaven. He reminds you about our Father's standards. He stands in the gap for you so that harm will not come your way. Trust Jesus, you know, you can tell Him everything and anything. He understands all that you have encountered. He cares about what you care about.

Trust, God the Holy Spirit. It is the voice on the inside that has always been there. It is a still small voice that talks to your heart to confirm, to warn and even to correct you. He reminds us of the Father's truth. He recalls buried memories. He nudges you towards godliness towards doing what is right. The Holy Spirit is like you being on a sailboat in the middle of nowhere alone. As you ask yourself what do I do? The wind then picks up the sail and it leads and directs, guides the boat (you) where it needs to go.

There is no failure in God. There is no way to walk with God except by trusting Him. There is no back up plan with God. He is your maker. Follow His lead even when things do not work out your way. Know that His way supersedes all of your plans. He is THE BOSS. The difference is He is not a dictator. He is a loving father, who always wants the best for your life which can and will always include Him. God's love is so overwhelming. He absolutely loves us. I did not really understand the depths of His love until He showed His footprints in my life, as He carried me when I was unable to walk or carry myself. I was too weak, too wounded, too fearful, too confused, so uncertain, and plain lost in need of my DADDY TO PICK ME UP AND CARRY ME!

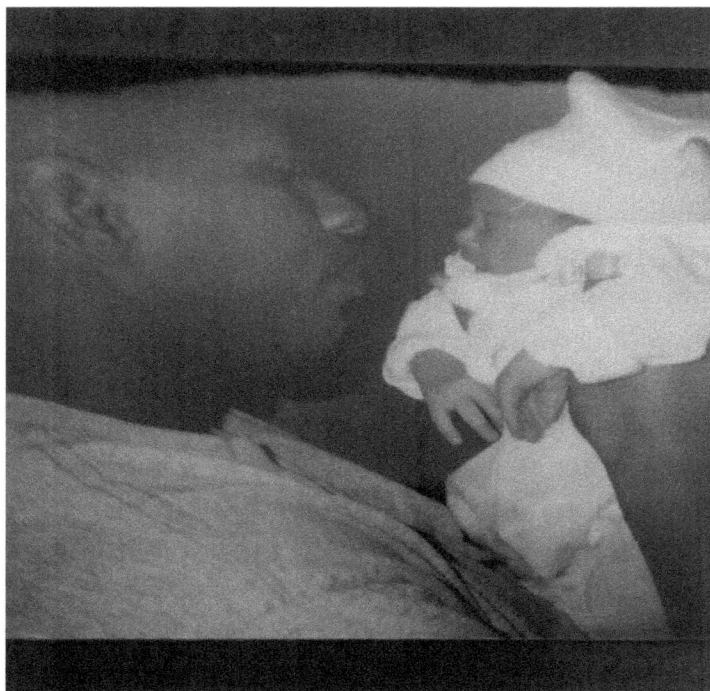

He did it! He gets all the Glory. God's Grace is Sufficient.

It is important to walk in His grace and not attempt to go it alone. If you do you will surely end up asking for God's help. Those that Do Not cast their cares to God find themselves getting frustrated, irritable, and confused. Neglecting to stand on His word will cause you to struggle unnecessarily.

2 Corinthians 9:8 (KJV): *And God is able to make ALL grace abound toward you; that ye, always having all sufficiency in all things, may abound to every good work.*

When sickness strikes- the Lord's grace is expedient to heal,
When resources are scarce- the Lord's grace will provide,
When faced with conflict-the Lord's grace reminds us that a solution was found over 2,000 years ago at the foot of Jesus's cross,
When uncertainty comes- the Lord's grace will provide clarity,
When a dark season falls on your life- realize the Lord's grace is just as visible there, regardless of your ability to see it.
When it seems that you are lacking something, boast in that weakness because this is exactly the area in which God will want to display His power and glory (in your finances, your marriage, your grades and the list goes on).

Think about it, even Jesus in His humanity was challenged with the same things that we face daily. When we walk in the flesh and not in the spirit you will too sweat great drops of blood just like Jesus in the Garden of Gethsemane. We sweat great drops of blood, doubts, fear, frustrations and at times experience feeling of hopelessness. When, we do not use God's grace, we face all that comes to battle your flesh. Instead be encouraged to know that Jesus came to himself and said to His father *"Not my will but YOUR will be done."* Jesus submitted to God's plan, angels came to minister to him, and Jesus was strengthened for the Journey to the cross. We are not meant to go it alone. We need God in everything that we do, from the least to greatest things in our lives. We have to FULLY RELY ON GOD- be the one that lives a life of a FROG- I am one who FULLY RELIES ON GOD.

1 Corinthians 1:27 says *But God chose the foolish things of the world to confound the wise and God has chosen the weak things of the world to shame the things which are strong.*

Psalm 23:4 says *Yea, though I walk through the valley of the shadow of death, I will fear no evil for thou art with me, thy rod, and thy staff they comfort me.*

"Yea /Yes means victory before the walk thru."

Ephesians 2:8-9 (NIV) *It is by grace you have been saved through faith and this is not from* *yourselves, it is a gift of God not by works so that no one can boast.*

God wants you to:

- Humble yourself,
- Ask God for Help - Then do what He says,
- Trust in His power- He is mighty to do whatever we need Him to help us to do.
- Trust in His wisdom- He knows what, when and how,
- Trust in His goodness- He loves you and has a plan for your life,

Now look back at His AMAZING Grace. It is simply amazing of how He has carried us through the most difficult times of our lives.

He is not like man. They will not last the distance. They may want something in return, some will reject you, some will leave you, some will talk about you, BUT HIS GRACE IS Sufficient. He is not like that. He will never leave or forsake us.

God is not asking us to endure our hardships. God is asking us to persevere, keep at it, to carry on, to stick with it, as we trust in his possibilities. In doing so, God will lift us above our circumstances as he develops our character.

When we begin to trust, we must also begin to forgive. Jesus commanded us to forgive or we will not be forgiven. It is not a choice, but it is a command. It does not seem fair, but forgiveness is the only way to truly live this life God's way. As unfortunate as it is, we will need to forgive others as well as be prepared for others to forgive us. No one is perfect. Even in our imperfections, we will need to move forward and the only way to totally free ourselves from past pains and hurts is we must release that pain with the power of forgiveness. Until you do it, you will remain in bondage. So, make a conscious decision to choose to forgive, Jesus did it while he was being murdered on the cross.

Luke 23:34 (AMP): *And Jesus prayed, Father, forgive them for they know not what they do*

Let us look to the powerful message that Christ continues to even teach and train God's people while yet dying on the cross. Jesus gave us His best sermon yet. You see Christ still interceding for man, while breathing
some
of his last breaths on the cross as He said Father forgive them. The gift of forgiveness is an intentional choice which is motivated by obedience to God. Look at Jesus, he was obedient until death. Even when refusal to forgive or bitterness can be justified by man, it can never be justified by God, because of Christs' ultimate sacrifice.

God's offered redemption at the cross, brings forgiveness which enables us to bless those who hurt us. Look at Jesus who showed us selflessly how he did not think of himself but instead was able to bless those who mocked him, who hated him, who tortured him even as they were in the process, Jesus showed true forgiveness.

Jesus the great teacher that he is, still instructs as He knows how to do to reveal unto man an intimate exchange of prayer as he talks to His Father. Jesus allowed us to ease drop on his conversation with his Father. Thank you, Jesus! He says Father forgive them for they know not what they do. Yes, even while dying, He shared history with us HIS STORY, HIS LOVE Story of redemption, the great atonement offered from son to father for man.

The SYMBOL (What Would Jesus Do) WWJD comes from this moment of Jesus showing us an intimate revelation of how a son talks to his Father while giving grace and having mercy upon those who were in the very act of murdering Christ. That grace and mercy was also extended to those who would come after (US) who sin against the will of God. Jesus' perfect example of love requires us to model our lives after Jesus. We are to imitate Christ rather than man. Do not get caught up in the drama of man making you bitter; instead, choose to follow Christ and become better. WWJD- He loved unconditionally, he demonstrated Gods' will by walking out the word in the flesh while he was here on earth.

We are cautioned not to be Bitter:

1. Refusing to forgive is a sin.
2. Bitterness damages your relationship with God.
3. Bitterness forgets hope, misdirects your focus.
4. Bitterness causes resentment, depression, and anger.
5. Bitterness is like an open wound that festers your soul. It alienates you from God and people.
6. Bitterness detours you from God's perfect plan for your life.

To Become Better and to be Able to Trust, You Must Forgive:

1. Forgiveness restores a right relationship with God for a more intimate love relationship.
2. Forgiveness allows you to release others from blame, thus allowing you to leave the hurt in God's hands as you choose to move on.
3. Forgiveness allows hope, peace, and love to be restored.

4. Forgiveness simply means I trust you God and I desire a clean heart.
5. Forgiveness gives us the ability to Thank God for having a 2nd chance.
6. Lastly Forgiveness is the beautiful gift given by God through Christ gives us eternal life.

Ephesians 4:31-32 (NIV) says *Get rid of all bitterness, rage, and anger, brawly and slander along with every form of malice. Be kind and compassionate to one another forgiving each other, just as in Christ, God forgave you.*

Remember that Christ demonstrated everything, and He did it all for you. He has overcome the world. Know that in the midst of his excruciating suffering, the heart of Jesus was focused on others rather than himself. Jesus not only suffered the pain of our wrongs, but also paid for their consequences in order that we may have forgiveness offered to us when we sin. The gift of forgiveness will change you from being bitter and it will make you better.

You have no choice when you say you are a child of the King. It is not easy and will sometimes require a process but press the start button of your life and move forward. Release those who hurt you, not for them but for yourself. Release resentment, release the spoken hurt, lies, and memories. You cannot do it alone, but you can do it with the love of Christ. Remember you are not your own, but you are an Ambassador of Christ.

I hear your heart saying: "The pressure was so much, I almost didn't make it, I almost lost my mind, it was too much to bear, I almost lost it all, you just don't understand!"

I say back to you, no one person will be able to understand completely what you went through, but Jesus does. He knows all about our pain, for He endured it all to save the lost.

Here is what the word tells you:

Choose godly friends:

Proverbs 27:17 *As iron sharpens iron, so a man sharpens the countenance of his friend.*

Isaiah 41:10 *Fear not, for I am with you, be not dismayed, for I am your God. I will strengthen you, Yes, I will help you. I will uphold you with my righteous right hand.*

Isaiah 43:18 and 25 *Do not remember the former things nor consider the things of old. Behold I will do a new thing.*

Joel 2:25-27 *So I will restore to you the years that the swarming locust has eaten, the cankerworm, and the caterpillar, and the palmerworm, my great army which I sent among you. You shall eat in plenty and be satisfied and praise the name of the Lord your God, who has dealt wondrously with you, and my people shall never be put to shame.*

Whatever you are going through make it at all costs to get to Jesus. Press in and thru and fall at His feet. Do not be easily offended. For offenses will keep you from the presence of God.

I GOT TO GET TO JESUS AT ALL COST!!!

Note: When God gives you a revelation you must respond to the new information. Get confirmation. God's promises are to be trusted and whatever He speaks becomes. So, speak those things that are not as though they would be.

Say out loud: God I Trust You." Make a declaration before the Lord by saying "every plan of God will be established. Every assignment and attack of the enemy will be destroyed."

Chapter 8:

Go Deeper- God Says Do You Trust Me? Are You All In?

Boat Dream

I recall a dream where the Master (The Lord) said to me jump in. There were also two others on the boat with me, but He instructed me to jump in. I said I cannot swim. But even still I jumped in and I sank deep in the ocean. Before I jumped in, I

remember feeling so scared. I faced my greatest fear. Even though I was scared I knew that I must be obedient. I remember thinking obedience even unto death, referring to Jesus and how He did everything His dad instructed him to do even unto death. So, I jumped thinking that I would die but I would also be with Christ. It was hard to understand but I did not allow myself the time or the ability to rationalize my instructions. Most things in Christ are not understood with the mind. They are felt by the heart. If God instructed me to jump, then there has to be something good coming out of my demise. I could not think anymore not one more second, so I jumped with fear, I jumped with hope, I jumped in obedience to my instruction from God. Yes, I jumped and as my body glided downward, I could see the images of people from below on the boat. The light shined brightly upon the boat from underneath in the dark beckoning waters. I did not recall gagging or grasping for breath I just felt the darkness consuming my being floating downward into the abyss. When I felt helpless and hopeless, a hand reached down into the place of darkness and pulled me up and out of the deep water. In spite of the depth, the darkness, and the uncertainty. I jumped because I knew that He never would leave or forsake me even in this.

God what does this mean? He shared with me from the inside that low He is always with me even to the ends of the earth. He reassured me that there is no place that God will not come to, to save us, help us, restore, and grace us with His almighty presence. He did not leave me alone. In my reluctant obedience, he honored my being all in. I spoke my inability to swim to the God that made me, just as Moses said I cannot talk eloquently to Pharaoh. God reminded Moses like He did with me, "who made man's mouth?" meaning that He made us and knows all about us more than we know ourselves. In our human inability, God meets us where we are and instructs us not to stay there in a place of fear, instead He compels us to come into our rightful place of being in Him. "I have a mind of Christ; therefore, I trust God."

2 Corinthians 12:10 Paul says ***"So I am well pleased with weaknesses, with insults, with distresses, with persecutions, and with difficulties, for the sake of Christ; for when I am weak (in human strength), then I am strong (truly able, truly powerful, truly drawing from God's strength)."***

Scripture: 2 Corinthians 12:9 (KJV). *And He said unto me "My grace is sufficient for thee: for my strength is made perfect in weakness. Most gladly therefore will I rather glory in my infirmities, that the power of Christ may rest upon me.*

Title: His Grace is Sufficient for me and you.

The word grace is found in the bible 159 times. Grace has been commonly defined as unmerited favor. Grace is God's ability working within man, making him able to do what he cannot do in his own ability. Grace is God's power coming to us freely as we put our faith in Him, enabling us to do with ease what we could never do on our own, without struggle or effort. Grace signifies the good will of God towards us and that is enough to enlighten and enliven us. God's grace is sufficient to strengthen. The word sufficient is defined as having or providing as much as is needed. You see God is El Shaddai "Almighty God," the One that is sufficient", "All sufficient Sustainer." You see in the text Paul is asking God to get rid of a physical or spiritual problem that he just wanted God to move, abolish, and destroy. God's answer to us is not always what we want to hear but is always what we need to hear. God's response to Paul was **"My Grace is sufficient."**

What is that thing in your life that you have dealt with for so long? What is that thing that has just been worrying you? What is that thing that you have asked God to take way? Well, whatever your thing is God has answered us all today, by sharing his conversation with Paul. That answer applies today, right now in your life and even in your neighbor's life. Gods' grace can handle anything. You will go up against the worst of circumstances and always come out on top. God's grace is victorious no matter what. You see the ability to accomplish God's tasks does not rely on our adequacy but on God's sufficiency. The text goes on to say that my **strength is made perfect in weakness. Perfect means having no mistakes or flaws, complete, correct, and accurate, exactly right for a particular purpose, situation, or person.**

You see God in His infinite wisdom, does things that we are unable to understand. God's way is not to take His children out of the trial, but to give them strength to bear up against it. Our human nature is to run and run fast to get far away from that thing that appears to be afflicting us. Yes, we saints have bound and loosed prayers of removal from situations or circumstances that were actually intended for our lives. Yes, bad things happen to good people. Look at what happened to Jesus He was Crucified bad. Resurrection gave God ultimate glory in the perfection of His beloved son. Daniel in the lion's den was bad. Deliverance from the lion's den gave God glory. Josephs'-Pit, Prison was bad the Palace gave God glory and saved a generation of God's people. So sometimes things may appear to come to take you out BUT GOD is always in control.

God has a purpose to not let us get the big head. He wants us to stay humble. All things work together for our good. God's intent is for us to be like His son Jesus. Pride besets a fall. God loves us, His will is to keep us from being exalted above measure; and spiritual burdens are ordered to cure spiritual pride. Prayer is a salve for every prayer is a strategy to every plan. Troubles are sent to teach us to pray and are meant to help us stay close to God with the idea to seek His counsel on how to navigate through and around the land mines of life.

It is important to walk in His grace and not attempt to go it alone. If you do you will surely end up asking for God's help. Those that do not cast their cares to God find themselves getting frustrated, irritable, and confused. Neglecting and learning how to stand with and for God, neglecting standing on His word will cause you to struggle unnecessarily- Tell your neighbor **because His Grace is sufficient.**

NOTE: INTIMACY with God (See into Me Lord) I know that I know. Trusting God will call you to private time with God in prayer. When you confront a problem, you must know that there is a prayer that you need to pray. Prayer is how we talk to God and how He talks back to us. God has an answer for it he says in **Jeremiah 33:3-** *Call upon me. I will answer and I will show you great and mighty things you know not of.* Trusting God, you must agree to be committed to the process.

God says in **Isaiah 41:10**, Fear not (there is nothing to fear), for I am with you, do not look around you in terror and be dismayed, for I am your God. I will strengthen and harden you to difficulties, Yes, I will help you; Yes, I will hold you up and retain you with My victorious right hand of righteousness and justice.

Knowing God means that you have had the opportunity or several opportunities for trusting God. You can only trust Him after you have seen Him show up on the scene of your life. You have gone through some hard stuff and you now know that your God is Greater and Bigger than that. Whatever your' that is, please know that God is Bigger. For He is the Almighty God. He is Elohim, El Shaddai.

God loves us so much that He preserves us. He comes after us. He searches for the one and leaves the ninety-nine. His love is without limits, it is without boundaries. His love went on the cross just for you.

While watching the Christian Television show called "Amazing Facts" Pastor Doug Batchelor shared this story which depicts Jesus' Redemption for Man.

Consider this story of a father who had two boys and they sailed on a boat and they crossed a certain section (pathway) on the ocean. The Father of the sons warned them about this particular spot with great caution. He instructed them not to ever snorkel or enter the water in this place, as it was known to be a place of many sharks, who sought just a drop of blood to feed. Well the boys took little caution to their father's warnings and began to play to where one son fell overboard, and they saw no activity in the water as they were warned. They even stated they had not seen one shark along the way. So, the other son jumped in too. As they played unaware of the warned danger, the father who was above on the highest point of the boat could see far, as the sons could not see the mounting danger. One dorsal fin appeared, and the father could see where the other sharks began to circle the unaware sons readying up for a kill.

The father is an instant thought that he had to save both of his sons immediately. So, he quickly ran and cut his wrist to draw blood and jumped in the water in the opposite direction where the boys were to distract the mounting sharks. He sacrificed his life to save his sons. From a distance the boys saw the sharks engaged in a feeding frenzy. They immediately got out of the water. Ultimately, they found out that their father willingly sacrificed his life to save theirs. What an overwhelming gift of love their good father gave to save them. It was such an incredible gift to give. So how do we receive it? As willingly as he gave, we receive. So simple, but so true. Just receive the God's gift to live a life in Him and with Him. So why would you stay in the water (in the world)? When you can get into God's boat of redemption. Jesus died so we can live. He died in our place. It should have been us that should have died, but God had a plan that He would take our place. So, get out and come in! You are welcome into the largest family ever known, The Kingdom of God. Consider you are now royalty. A child of the King.

Trusting God means that in spite of it all, He gave me the grace to stay with it all, to overcome it all. I wanted God to save me and take me out of this, but His divine favor was upon me and His grace was sufficient. He did not take me out of the problem but instead He helped me walk through it to show His glory. I grew in the middle of evil, selfish, and ungodly people. I was built for this. I grew and matured in the midst of dirty people, dirty places, and dirty things. Yes, a rose grows out of dirt. God uses dirt to grow beauty.

Isaiah 61:3 *³To appoint unto them that mourn in Zion, to give unto them beauty for ashes, the oil of joy for mourning, the garment of praise for the spirit of heaviness; that they might be called trees of righteousness, the planting of the LORD, that he might be glorified.*

Through it all, every story, every trial, every struggle, and every loss, I only endured it because of God's Amazing Love. Look at what I get every time, "I get more God." I have learned to love Him even the more, to appreciate the shared grace and mercy on my life, to know that no matter how wrong I am, how low I go, He is always right there to pick me up, to correct me, to protect me and above all to LOVE ME. "He Loves Me! Yes, He loves You, YES YOU!!!"

Chapter 9:

Trust Means Becoming Dependent On God

Trust Rules Out being independent and instead leads you to become Dependent on God. God orders my steps. He guides me and provides His wisdom daily. His mercies are new every day. I have been developed to go through, all the way through to my breakthrough. Break me into those places that will not submit to your word and will. **Break me in to go through to get to you.**

NOTE: Trust God specially to overcome: Hatred, slander, disappointment, revenge, retaliation against enemies and unwillingness to forgive.

God will bless you to release yourself from the lies of the enemy and from wrong thinking. Do good and give God your best every day in every way. Trust allows your wounds to heal and become battle scars. Having a battle scar says that you Got the victory and God Got the glory. This will allow the healing process to happen. There is vulnerability in healing. There is also hope in trusting God. Tell yourself, I will not always be in this place. I will not stay wounded. Instead, I choose by faith to be free and healed. You may say "I don't trust anyone!" well I say to you, keep people in their right place. God is always first. Try a spirit by a spirit. Look for their fruit. Do not just blindly give away your trust without asking God who you can lean on. Remember that at some point, no one person can be all that you need or want because honestly people will fall and fail. They are mere men. So be wise and count on the all wise God who will direct your path. **Ask, Seek and Knock (Matthew 7:7).**

Church Hurt, Spiritual Manipulation and Religious Control

If you are serving within the body of Christ, please know that God is well aware of all that is around you. Never become so comfortable with taking man's words above the word of God. See and hear with your spiritual eyes. Seek God daily as to who is of and for God. You need to know that wolves are dressed in sheep's clothing disguised as people of God, but their hearts are far from it. Use godly discernment and be obedient to God's voice. For a stranger's voice they will not follow. Follow the good shepherd, Follow Jesus.

GOD, FAMILY, CHURCH

NOT

CHURCH, FAMILY, GOD

Unhealthy Habits become Ungodly Decisions

Let not your works falsely pursue the glory of God. God will show you the hearts of men and women that you serve with. Ask that their motives be revealed. As God shows you their true hearts, do not be angry and disappointed because your Father in heaven has heard your prayers and loves enough to give you a revelation. Do not allow acts of service, loyalty to the pastor and ministry, wearing certain clothing, and church talk be mistaken as faithfulness. Instead look for the purity of heart. God will reveal the heart of those who labor amongst. Tell God thank you for showing you the truth, for the truth shall set you free. Do not allow a genre of church, a denomination, a type of people, a leadership title lead you astray. Just because a place is familiar does not mean that you belong there. Those things matter but what truly matters is your heart before the King. You can never do enough. God does not need our works. His love is a wonderful gift. All you have to do is just accept it. For He sees the heart of man. He knows our thoughts and not just our actions. He sees the motive behind the heart of a man. Honor authority by honoring the position and not the person. God is a jealous God and beside Him there is no other. No one comes before God. So, do not be deceived. God will show you. Keep asking and when He answers, be obedient.

Proverbs 26:24-25 *He who hates pretends with his lips but stores up deceit within himself. When he speaks kindly, do not trust him, for seven abominations are in his heart.*

Chapter 10:

Pursuit of Purpose

- Be intentional when pursuing God's plan.
- Transition is necessary in order to move forward.
- Move step by step forward by trusting God.
- Step out of fear and step into Faith.
- Trust God more than you trust your feelings.
- The "what if's" have no place in our lives. We are to know and have confidence in Him, NOT in the thing, the person or place. We are to trust in Him (totally and completely).
- Trust and say "YES" to God in His purpose and in His Plan.
- Trust God and Step out. He will meet you there. He has always been there for you.
- Do not allow desires to define your purpose.
- God is not surprised by your mistakes. He has not changed His mind about you. For He loves us unconditionally. His love is limitless, endless, and never changing. He will use my mistakes and create a masterpiece with my life to put on display for His Glory.

Suppression is not Surrender

Merriam-Webster's dictionary states to Suppress means the following....
1: to put down by authority or force, **2**: to keep from public knowledge: such as **a**: to keep secret **b**: to stop or prohibit the publication or revelation of **3a**: to exclude from consciousness **b**: to keep from giving vent to **4** *obsolete*: to press down **5a**: to restrain from a usual course or action

Suppress Synonyms

belie, blanket, blot out, cloak, conceal, cover, curtain, disguise, enshroud, hide, mask, obscure, occult, paper over, screen, shroud, veil

Merriam- Webster's dictionary states to Surrender means the following... **a**: to yield to the power, control, or possession of another upon compulsion or demand, **b**: to give up completely or agree to forgo especially in favor of another, **2a**: to give (oneself) up into the power of another especially as a prisoner, **b**: to give (oneself) over to something (such as an influence): to give oneself up into the power of another

Surrender Synonyms: Verb
bow, cave (in), give in, submit, succumb, yield

Surrender Synonyms: Noun

capitulating, capitulation, cession, handover, relinquishment, rendition, submission, submitting

When we suppress our inner feelings, we hold back unresolved pain. The pressure mounts up over time. Sometimes the pressure relieves itself in painful ways. God wants to help you surrender your painful past and look to Him. Trusting all that you have gone through has a greater purpose than your right now pain.

Release, surrendering can be a long process. It depends on how bad you want to be healed. Facing unpleasant truths, acknowledging the hidden sin (especially unresolved generational curses) can hinder or delay your greatness in God.

Suppression looks to others like everything is okay and says that you are fine and have adjusted. But in fact, you know the truth and your words are far away from what is actual or factual. You have told yourself that "If I bury it, if I don't think about it, it will go AWAY." Yes, you begin to believe the lie, telling yourself you will be okay, you can handle it. Until you are hit with a trigger. Anything and Everything closes in on you. A simple gesture, an unexpected touch or a simple word phrase starts the emotions to overflow. Your mind has gone backwards into a rabbit hole that you may never come out of. Your breathing becomes labored. It hits you right in your gut just like it did back then.

You ask yourself, "how could this happen to me? Why did this happen to me? Can anyone see or feel my pain? I am feeling like I am dying. Help me! I am drowning on the inside of my heart. Please help me, please take the pain, and hurt away. I cannot do this anymore. I need real help. Not empty kind words, not anything. I just need you, Lord. I cannot breathe! They are taking away my kids. No, No, No, No!!!!!!!!!!!! I cannot breathe! How do I stop this from happening? Can anyone help me? Lord, I do not know what to do. I hurt, I ach, I bleed. I am overwhelmed!"

Somehow in the midst of the deepest pain and hurt, I mustarded up enough strength to begin to declare and decree my finish from the beginning. I spoke to Fear and I said at the top of my voice while weeping that "God didn't give me the spirit of Fear, but of love, power and sound mind. No! No! No! No! Weapon that is formed against me shall prosper and every tongue that rises will be condemned by you. The LORD is my shepherd; I shall not want. He maketh me to lie down in green pastures: he leadeth me beside the still waters. He restoreth my soul: He leadeth me in the paths of righteousness for his name's sake. Yea, though I walk through the valley of the shadow of death, I will fear no evil: for thou art with me; thy rod and thy staff they comfort me Thou preparest a

table before me in the presence of mine enemies: thou anointest my head with oil; my cup runneth over. Surely goodness and mercy shall follow me all the days of my life: and I will dwell in the house of the LORD forever."

Rivers of living water began to flow out of my belly. I began to speak to the situation and not let the situation speak to me. I told the devil get behind me because I will be victorious no matter what. I stood and therefore stood with the word of God until the physical yielded to God's perfect will for my life. I spoke to the storm and The Mighty God that I serve gave me victory and He Got all the glory.

WHAT DO YOU DO WHEN YOU CAN'T GO ANY FURTHER, LISTEN ANYMORE, WHEN YOU CAN'T HEAR NOT ONE MORE WORD? LORD WHAT DO I DO WHEN I GET TIRED, WEARY AND UNSETTLED?

My prayer:

Lord, help me to love the unlovable, help me to trust you the more, in spite of what I deal with. Lord I trust you. Help me to trust others you place in my life. May I not harm them. May I speak life even when I don't want to. Let your thoughts, your words replace my ungodly thoughts. Deliver me from going backwards. Help heal, recover, and restore all broken areas in my life, in my mind, in my heart, in my spirit and in my soul. Touch it all. Do not leave anything undone. In Jesus name, Amen.

In the middle of the most horrific experience of my life, I felt the ultimate strength of God. I was battered, broken, and wounded but the God of my salvation heard my cry and lifted me out of my pit. I felt the suppression and oppression of the enemy trying to take my life, my sanity, and my family BUT GOD came to my rescue. He sheltered me, He protected me, He covered me. I surrendered it all to the Mighty Hand of God.

Chapter 11:

Access Is Granted.........

John 14:6 says *Jesus said to him, I am the way, the truth, and the life. No one comes to the Father except through Me.*

John 14: 13 -15 - *And whatever you ask in my name, that I will do, that the Father may be glorified in the Son. "If you ask anything in my name, I will do it. "If you love me, keep my commandments.*

YOUR ACCESS HAS BEEN GRANTED

The word Access is defined as permission, liberty, or ability to enter, or communicate with a person or thing. You see we have access to so many things. Ask yourself are we truly connected to the right things in our lives? We are connected to titles. We are connected to certain groups or organizations or even to certain people with unseen motives. Our true access must first begin with our relationship with God. More specifically it is established by allowing Jesus the Christ to become our Lord and Savior. For the word of God clearly identifies the absolute distinction made by Jesus himself as He began to explain to his disciples how to connect with His Father in heaven. He identified how to gain access to the Master of the Universe. Very clearly and pragmatically he stated the only way to the Father is through the Son. You see the Son, Jesus through the resurrection has granted us access to the Kingdom of Heaven. The Kingdom of Heaven is not for just friends or associates but is the reward to the joint heirs to the kingdom of God. Our Father in Heaven, so desires for His children to have His absolute best. God's best will amaze and astound the average mind. You see the Father in Heaven, the son, Jesus, and the Holy Spirit all empower us to experience His greatness once we are obedient to His Will, His Word, and His Way.

God sent me by to tell somebody that **YOUR ACCESS HAS BEEN GRANTED!** God wants to bless us right here on earth. Your access was granted over 2000 years ago, we are God's anointed and appointed children, who need to walk in the authority that has been given unto us. Verse: 14 says if you ask in my name, I will do it. Our direct connection to Jesus Christ directs our path on the way to God's Holy Truth, by way of His Holy Word. When we listen, we gain access to external life. Yes, Jesus said that He is the way, the Truth, and the Life.

YOUR ACCESS HAS BEEN GRANTED.

This Access granted through Jesus is like having **an invisible backpack** which is complete with special provision, favor, blessed assurance, maps to your intended future, Jesus as your personal guide and the ability to speak in coded Holy Ghost tongues that the enemy can't decipher. This invisible knapsack carries your peace that surpasses all understanding. This invisible provision clothes the naked, gives food to the hungry and provides emergency gear in a time of crisis. Yes, this invisible backpack of provision writes checks in a time of financial need. You see this access opens closed doors and pours out blessings you will not have room to receive. **YOUR ACCESS HAS BEEN GRANTED!**

Come and see a Man. Jesus, you know him, the man who walked on water. The one who suffered the cross and broke the curse of death with His resurrection on the third day. You know the same Jesus who was blameless yet died for yours and my own sins. I am talking about the King of Kings. The Lord of Lords, who never sleeps nor slumbers. My Jesus is your Jesus. The same Jesus who loves you so dearly, also desires to give you God's best with His limitless love. Who could have ever shown a greater love than the man who laid down his life, for the lives of his brothers and sisters? There is no other. There is only ONE. He is our intercessor, who lightens the pathway to God. He is the one who reveals God's truth through our daily walk with Him. He is the one, who grants us access to eternal life. Yes, He is truly the way, the truth, and the life. Jesus implies that if you absolutely love him, provision will be given, to those who prove their devotion by their consistent obedience. If we diligently keep God's word, this obedience yields the presence of God in every situation of our lives. Obedience provides the access to daily provision.

Be reminded that Jesus did it all for you. We were all given an unearned advantage, a special entitlement that allows us access to the closed places that only could have been opened by Jesus, the Son of the Living God. Remember, be encouraged, and begin to speak God's word into your life with the power and authority given unto us through Jesus. You too can have the invisible knapsack of provision. Remember **YOUR ACCESS HAS BEEN GRANTED**.

Trusting God means arresting bitterness and resentment against those who hurt you. God does place people in our lives that are godly, trustworthy, truthful, honest, and on fire for God.

Test the Spirit by the Spirit. You will know them by their fruit. No matter what title they hold, what position they have or what they call themselves. Trust only those who live for God. You will know it. You will see it. God will show you Himself in their lives. Revenge is mine thus says the Lord. Trust that God is the judge and He alone. He will recompense. God's love is UNSTOPPABLE. It takes courage to take the first step, to move towards those who are for Christ. You are called to relationship. **JUST BE YOU!!!**

Chapter 12:

Trusting Again "How Can I Do That?"

I have asked the same question; I know I will again. I know I can but how do I get there? How do I move from NO Trust to a Little Trust to Great Trust? Complete Trust belongs only to God and not to man.

Ask yourself, how do I trust again? Well it will be a daily task and you yourself do not have the ability to do it alone. It can only be done with help from the Lord. You see the Holy Spirit within will heal the deep wounds. Trust develops, matures, and grows with consistent and patient love. When trust has been misplaced, or misused, the only way is to feel your way with the conviction of the Holy Spirit. Honestly, you must continue to try the spirit by the spirit. A real change will be consistent but cannot be perfect. Do not put people in places they ought not to be in.

Malachi 3:18 *Then you shall again discern between the righteous and the wicked, between who serves God and one who does not serve Him. Matthew 7:15-17. Beware of false prophets, who come to you in sheep's clothing, but inwardly* *they are ravenous wolves. You will know them by their fruits. Do men gather grapes from thorn bushes or figs from thistles? Even so every good tree bears good fruit, but a bad tree bears bad fruit."*

Prayer: Lord I humbly come to you giving you thanks. Lord I pray that Candace decreases as you increase, let your people see none of me, but all of you. Let the words of my mouth and the meditation of my heart be acceptable in thy sight, my Lord, my strength, and my redeemer. Lord let your anointing fall in this place. Lord let lives be changed, let hearts be encouraged. Lord I take authority over every demonic spirit and any plot or plan that would hinder your word from coming forth. Let your word be unhindered and uninterrupted. In Jesus Name, I pray Amen.

You Betta Test That Spirit!

Discernment or the "Discerning of Spirits", is a gift given by the power of the Holy Spirit. He bears witness to our spirit when something is not of God. Discernment is a gift used to detect the spirit realm and its activities. Spiritual eyes are opened and given supernatural revelation of the enemy's plots and plans. The gift of discernment is meant to protect and to guard the body of believers. How is it, that even the elect can be deceived? The testing of the spirits was not effectively done.

How to Test a Spirit?

1. **Observe what a person does.** Watch and pray, do not just let people get close until they have been tested. Time is healer and a revealer; this means that a true heart will be revealed in time. Saints need to be on guard, using their ability to offer surveillance to and for leadership and well as for yourself and those you love, your family. Protect and Serve. Watch for their conduct and actions in and out of the Body of Christ. Believe what their lives show you, do not be deceived if they something that does not line up with what they do.

2. **Observing whether or not a person exalts Christ, the Son of the Living God.** Jesus is the Way, the Truth, and the Light. You will see the fruit of the Spirit: Love, joy, peace, longsuffering, etc... The contrary is seeing the fruits of evil, gossip, envy, strife, jealousy etc....

3. **Listen to the words that come out of their mouths.** - Do comments show the example of Christ, even when joking or just having fun? Do words line up with God's written word? The truth will be revealed in a word, by their actions and by their deeds.

We perish for lack of Knowledge. Discernment is strengthened with prayer, by asking for increase of the gift, by reading and learning God's word and by walking in the Spirit. An acute sensitivity to the Holy Spirit will reveal the thoughts and the intent of a persons' heart, the true motives behind a given action. The urgency to pray and ask for wisdom, will allow the saints to be able to see the good in others. Follow your gut, it is really the Holy Ghost talking to you.

Discernment is used to help the Body Christ, to settle disputes, for counseling, spiritual warfare and especially for leadership. The judgmental or self-righteous spirit often accompanies the spirit of pride. Do not let the spirit of pride block the gift of discernment by causing a saint to think the gift is for personal gain or selfish motives. Do not deceive yourself, you must always consult with God for His purpose, His wisdom, and His understanding. God wants His believers to read between the lines and to find the truth in every situation. God empowers His people to unmask false prophets, religious spirits, familiar spirits, carnal spirits, and hypocrites. Discernment allows us to be able to see the deceivers who would otherwise appear to be genuine. True discernment seeks to protect God's people.

Strange things have happened. It happened to me. I felt that I let myself down because I allowed my former Pastor to become more than he needed to be in and over my life. It was not obvious at first but with time, newly found wisdom and by walking closer with God, He opened my blinded eyes. I began to see religious deception and manipulation. I honestly understood now where I judged others before, who belonged to cults. It did not start off that way, it was a gradual process coaxed with mentorship, encouragement and with a motive. I often heard, "If I were you, I would…" these recommendations, strong suggestions coupled with a father-like heart made to feel like love, were pure coercion. My mind simply became stuck for years, as I had a hard time believing that this spiritual and physical father figure had a motive that was not just for my good, but more so for his own personal benefit. Money, in the form of my tithes and financial support. Wow! Yes, I said it, "Money." I have had to ask the Holy Spirit to replace wrong thinking, stinking thinking with God's word and godly wisdom. The change took some time and to be honest, it was time that I desperately needed alone with God so that He could rebuild me. He began telling me how much He loved me and no matter what people may say, He will never leave or walk out on me. He will never let me down. He will support me when others forsake me. He answered me and showed me how to trust again and to strictly trust Him completely.

God and I had conversations where I would freely ask, "How could I have been misled, misguided, and hood winked like this, for so long?" I guess some of this connection was driven from my inner need to finally belong and be loved by this father figure, as my biological father had never done. As my biological father did not acknowledge my very existence until a few years ago. Yes, I am 51 and did not formerly have the protection, nurture, love, or support of a good faithful father. As God had it to be, I was still blessed with a wonderful mother who sacrificed daily to ensure I had above my needs. She is Awesome! God has since then healed my heart about not having my biological father's name on my birth certificate. God told me that I was His daughter and Hid name is parents written on my heart and the world would know that I belong to Him and Him alone. What a wonderful revelation for all of those who have didn't have to own you, or were rejected because of selfishness; please find comfort that you are not alone…GOD adores you and is glad to call you His child. Rejection of man is often times God way of protecting us from those who would not or could not value you as a gift. So, tell God thank you for protecting you from things you could not even begin to imagine would harm you. "Thank You, Jesus!!!"

Trusting my former spiritual leader made me realize that, he was not who he said he was. This revelation hit me to my core. The level of manipulation was strategic and demonstrative. Deep on the inside, it did not feel right. The words spoken did not match or fit with my spirit man. Now I know that my rightful and righteous father is only one, God the Father. Because inwardly I was searching for a father, coercion found itself in private leadership conversations, moments and/or chastisement that was unwarranted, non-biblical and plain ole wrong. Some leadership training sessions were intermixed with sound and personal doctrine, which was not Holy Ghost lead. When I heard it, it just felt wrong and I felt bad about myself. God was talking to me as I was so confused. I believed that this was disciplined spiritual development and because it did not feel right meant that I had more work to do. You see the lies began to penetrate. The only recognizable lesson that I will forever remember is that I must get confirmation in my spirit from the Holy Spirit. Boy, did I learn a valuable lesson.

I recall having conflicting thoughts that made me sound judgmental and who would believe or agree with what I was feeling on the inside. Who would believe that this man, my former spiritual father, was not being led by God? The wrestling that I experienced was in fact against the spirit of control. This spirit formerly made things mandatory as a way of monitoring and maintaining self-righteous ungodly religious control. I would

often whisper to God, "Lord help me."
Nevertheless, I still grew spiritually. I began to
seek God the more and through a series of dreams,
God would always show me what to pray for or
against. To this day, I battle with trusting ministry,
but I know that God is not locked up in a church
made from brick and mortar. Instead He resides in
my heart. Therefore, if you feel or felt trapped
know that God will direct your path.

Someone asked the question when my family
decided to leave that ministry, "Why did you stay
so long?" My family stayed for 15 years. The first
question was easy to answer. God showed me in a
series of dreams, what I should do. I grew in the
mist of darkness. Flowers grow while in dirt. I
emerged towards God's faithful light. He
protected me, covered me, and watered me and
when it was His time, He repotted me so I could
truly bloom all the more.

Back to trusting, my trusting is established in God.
I pray about everything and because I pray, God
answers. He always answers. I have learned to ask
about certain people and certain situations. He
confirms or denies my inquiries.

MY DREAM…

One night I dreamt about a python snake
restricting my entire body. The dream revealed the
spirit that I was battling with was exceptionally

large and that I needed help to be free to live and not to die. God reassured me that my help was on the way. Shortly after the dream I received my true release. My worship, my prayer life and my freedom in spirit was mocked, talked about and I was ostracized, BUT GOD. He heard me and freed me. God gave instructions and I followed. Trusting God is like nothing else I have ever experienced in my life. He has never let me down. He loves everything about me. He is so kind and sweet to me. He has never nor will He ever forsake me.

The way God makes me feel is like no other. His loving kindness is simply amazing and incomprehensible. It is indescribable. I stand in awe of Him. Yes, this is churchy, if the Lord had not been on my side where would I be?

NOTE: I See You Shouting with Me.

If you want to truly trust, begin with falling AWAY from being strong by yourself, for yourself and end up falling INTO the waiting arms of a loving Father who guards, guides, protects and restores.

I trust God when I am scared and fearful.

I trust God when I am angry.

I trust God when I just do not know what to do.

I trust God when others forsake me.

When I am mocked or misunderstood, **I trust God.**

When I need healing, **I trust God.**

I trust God because He is the one person who loves me like no other.

He is the one who encourages my purpose when others do not understand.

He stands with me and for me as my constant intercessor.

He loves me when others hate me.

God celebrates me in all things that represents Him.

God corrects me when others will agree just to agree even when I am wrong.

God is my Best Friend, my Chief and Commander, my Sole Protector, my Healer, my Deliverer, my Comforter, my Peace that surpasses all understanding. He is the Lover of my Soul.

Simply said, "I TRUST GOD!"

Chapter 13:

REMEMBER TO MOUNT UP!

God enables us to mount upward from failure, from let downs, from put downs and from miscalculations of life.

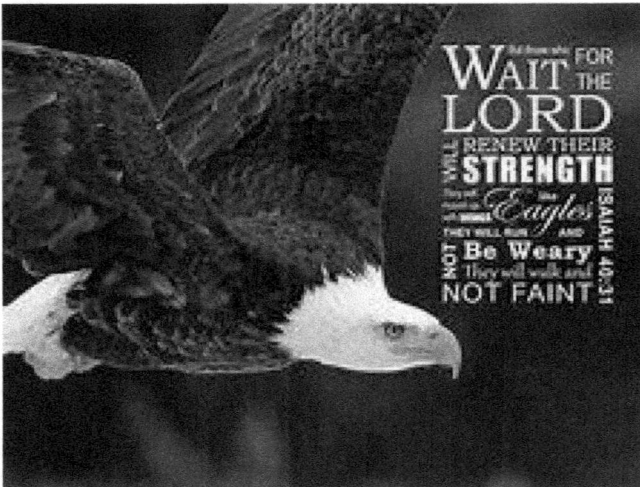

Isaiah 40:31 says *"But they that wait upon the Lord shall renew their strength; they shall mount up with wings as eagles; they shall run, and not be weary; and they shall walk, and not faint."*

"Mount Up with Wings Like an Eagle"

ISAIAH 40:21-31

The 40th chapter of Isaiah provides comfort for God's people. The verses clearly describe a God that we stand in awe of. He is our God who made all that we see and we at times take Him for granted. God made the heavens. God made the earth. God made the stars in the sky and the movement of the river's channels and its currents. He is the one who carved the Grand Canyon. He is the one and only who made man and mans' greatest abilities. Yes, God did it! Yes, God did it! All miracles, signs and wonders come from the mind of a Perfect, Holy and Righteous God. In this chapter God uses the prophet Isaiah to remind the people of Israel who He is. In knowing who God is, you will begin the journey of knowing who you are especially when you have connected to His son Jesus. We stand in awe of Him but are unable to truly be a child of the most- high God until we accept His son Jesus Christ. Once that connection is made, look out for the many ways, the many blessings that God will allow to come your way. Many have heard this familiar scripture that says Mount up with wings like eagles. The Eagle is a majestic, regal, and powerful bird that is viewed by many to signify strength and power because of its stature and its wings span. God's creation often times will show us His glory in the makeup of a majestic bird such as the eagle. The United States, the Eagle Scouts and many other organizations have followed God's lead and have identified the prominent characteristics of an eagle to define themselves. For many years, people have symbolized the eagle as a symbol of beauty, bravery, courage, honor, pride, determination, and grace. In the scripture the term mounts up is used to describe very plainly the majestic flight pattern of this mighty bird. To mount up means to set or place at an elevation. To increase in amount or intensity, to rise or go to a higher position, level, or degree. To ascend. Let us look at the life of an eagle.

MOUNT UP AND FLY LIKE AN EAGLE.

- Eagles are reported to be high-flyers. In order to fly high, you must have a good and positive attitude towards life. No matter what others may do or even say, it is your responsibility to fly above the negativity and doubt causing hindrances. Stay away from those who find it easy to complain; they are not focused on being God-minded. Never complain instead find good in everything that you encounter and just tell God "Thank you." A thankful heart pleases the Lord. Be who God has called you to be, a solution finder, one who listens to the guidance and godly wisdom of the Holy Spirit.
- Eagles know who they are. They will only be around like-minded individuals who

honor God and value the gifts that only God could have imagined and created within their lives. Eagles recognize their self-worth and value and are adamant about being exactly who they are created to be.

- It is said that we should have Eagles eyes. Why, because their strong vision allows them to see far, far away. Are you able to discern or see things far before it comes close? It is important to improve your ability to see. That is called discernment. We are to detect the activities of the enemy before he launches an attack. We can counter every attack because we are equipped spiritually. For us, our Holy Spirit radar will detect the enemy from way off. When an eagle sites his prey, he narrows his focus on it and sets out to get it. No matter the obstacles, the eagle will not move his focus from the prey until he grabs it. Remain focused on Christ. The eagle is known to be a patient bird. We need to wait on the Lord and the Lord's appointed time to get every blessing that He has in store for his children. The ability to see far comes from our super put on our natural! We must be led by the Holy Spirit to stay in God's divine order for His purpose and His glory. Have a vision and remain focused no matter what the obstacle and you will succeed.

- Just like the Eagle, God equips us uniquely to run to things that others will run away from. The military, firefighters and EMS workers are those who possess the understanding some situations may be considered dangerous and will still run towards the danger merely, because it is just what needs to be done. They just do it, unapologetically. Each storm in life is meant to groom you and grow you. Let the storms of Life be viewed as a hidden opportunity disguised in a seemingly overwhelming obstacle. So, do not avoid the storms but instead grow in them. We can use the storms of life to rise to greater heights. Use the storm as a place that will benefit you once the challenge is dealt with.
- Just like Eagles do, we must test our relationships before we choose to trust. Never follow others in blind obedience, instead be led by God. If you are following the instructions of another and it is not GOD, then you are spiritually BLIND. Repent and ask God to forgive you. He is faithful to forgive and then get your new Holy Ghost marching orders and do not turn left or right unless He tells you to. Know who you labor amongst. Before you call someone a friend, allow the Lord to show you who they truly are by learning what is on the inside of their hearts. Whether in your

private life or in business, we should always test the level of commitment that an individual has towards an intended connection or partnership.

- It is God's family design that both male and female eagles participate in raising their eagle family. It indeed takes a 'Village" to raise a god-centered family. Those who offer support must be God and Kingdom minded, as it takes more than active parents to properly teach, train and nurture children. Only receive help/support from those who you have prayed about and God has confirmed their connection to your family. It is also important that a new season will require you to get a fresh and updated word from God about those who are close to your family. Please do not assume just because they are family or if you have known them all your life that they are allowed to move forward with you into God's plan for your life. "Test that Spirit."

- As the eagles build their nest, we should be reminded that we should always prepare ourselves for change. The preparation for the family teaches us that active participation of both partners leads to success. Some nests are intentionally designed to include thorns around the exterior used a protective measure to ensure the family is safe within as well as used to ensure the enemy is kept out for added security.

NOTE to Parents/Caregivers: It is our God-given responsibility to protect those that God has entrusted unto us. So, do your job, "It's okay to say, "NO! or to check out references even when things may appear on the surface to look good. Everything that is good, isn't always God, but everything that is God is always good!"

Change most of the time can be painful, but we need to get rid of old things that just do not work anymore. We must get rid of unpleasant memories, bad habits and fixed mindsets that will hinder God's growth and development. We must die unto ourselves in order for God to get His best out of us. Can you imagine how much God can do in our lives if we would simply enter into the secret place and allow the better to come forth?

MOUNT UP, MOUNT UP.

The sky is the limit with God when we let Him be God. We can mirror our characteristics after the courageous, powerful majestic bird called the eagle. So be all that God has called you to be. MOUNT UP like with the wings of an Eagle. Run on do not be weary. God will give you strength if you wait on the Lord.

Romans 8: 28 says *"And we know that all things work together for good to those who love God, to those who are called according to His purpose."*

Chapter 14:

The Law of Forgiveness Means Trusting God

Luke 23:34 (AMP): *And Jesus prayed, Father, forgive them for they know not what they do. And they divided His garments and distributed them by casting lots for them.*

Title of Message: Follow Christ's Example of The Gift of Forgiveness

Short Version: Christ wants to move you from being, Bitter to being Better!

Let us look to the powerful message where Christ continues to teach and train God's people while yet dying on the cross. Jesus gave us His best sermon yet. You see Christ is still interceding for man, while breathing some of his last breaths on the cross. He said Father forgive them. The gift of forgiveness is an intentional choice which is motivated by obedience to God. Look at Jesus, he was obedient unto death. Even when un-forgiveness or bitterness can be justified by man, it can never be justified by God, because of Christs' ultimate sacrifice. God's offering redemption on the cross, brings forgiveness which enables us to bless those who hurt us. Look at Jesus who showed us selflessly how he did not think of himself but instead was able to bless those who mocked him, who hated him, who tortured him even as they were in the process, Jesus showed true forgiveness.

Jesus the great teacher that he is still instructs as He knows to do, to reveal unto man an intimate exchange of prayer as he talks to His Father. Jesus allowed us to ease drop on his conversation with his Father. Thank you, Jesus. He says, "Father forgive them for they know not what they do." Yes, even while dying, He shared history with us HIS STORY, HIS LOVE story of redemption, the great atonement offered from son to father for man.

The SYMBOL WWJD comes from this moment of Jesus showing us an intimate reveal of how the son talks to His Father giving grace and mercy upon those who were in the very act of murdering Christ but was also extended to those who would come after (US) who sin against the will of God. Jesus' perfect example of love requires us to model our lives after Jesus. We are to imitate Christ rather than imitating Man. Do not get caught up in the drama of Man making you bitter; instead, choose to follow Christ and become better. WWJD- He loved unconditionally, he showed Gods' will by demonstrating the word in the flesh while he was here on earth.

WE ARE CAUTIONED NOT TO BE BITTER:

Ephesians **4**:31 Let all **bitterness** and wrath **and anger** and clamor and slander be put away from you, along with all malice.

1. Refusing to forgive is a sin.
2. Bitterness damages your relationship with God.
3. Bitterness forgets hope, misdirects your focus.
4. Bitterness causes resentment, depression, and anger.
5. Bitterness is like an open wound that festers in your soul.
6. Bitterness alienates you from God and people.
7. Bitterness detours you from God's perfect plan for your life.

> Be kind to one another,
> *tenderhearted,*
> forgiving one another,
> as God in Christ
> *forgave you.*
>
> [Ephesians 4:32]

To Become Better You Must Forgive:

1. Forgiveness restores a right relationship with God for a more intimate love relationship.
2. Forgiveness allows you to release others from blame, thus allowing you to leave the hurt in God's hands as you choose to move on.
3. Forgiveness allows hope, peace, and love to be restored.
4. Forgiveness simply means I trust you God and I desire a clean heart.
5. Forgiveness gives us the ability to Thank God for having a 2nd chance.
6. Lastly Forgiveness is the beautiful gift given by God through Christ gives us eternal life.

Ephesians 4:31-32 (NIV) says Get rid of all bitterness, rage, and anger, brawling and slander along with every form of malice. Be kind and compassionate to one another forgiving each other, just as in Christ God forgave you. Remember that Christ showed and did it all for you. He has overcome the world. Know that in the midst of his excruciating suffering the heart of Jesus was focused on others rather than himself. Jesus not only suffered the pain of our wrongs, but also paid for their consequences in order that we may have forgiveness offered to us when we sin. The gift of forgiveness will change you from being bitter and it will make you better. **God wants to change you from bitter to better!** THE LAW OF FORGIVENESS means trusting God. Did you know that stubbornness is a form of idolatry, which pushes back against the will of God?

Trust God with forgiveness. Yes, I trust God's way, as He gives me the ability to forgive those who have deeply hurt and wounded me. No, I do not want to but here is where I trust God in a different way; I trust that His ways are higher than my own ways. God commands us to forgive, if you recall Jesus forgave us all to include those at Cavalry that did their best to kill Jesus. While being crucified, He forgave those who hurt Him dearly, so If Jesus did, I must do the same.

You may have said it with your mouth, and it did not get to your heart. Remember that your head will always rationalize and justify what the flesh wants to do. The flesh does not and will not forgive. Tell yourself that my head is not he boss of me, but I am led by the Holy Spirit and although it may be difficult it is not impossible to do. I will forgive but not in my own strength but in the strength of God. Trusting God means that I will not always feel this way if I make a conscious decision to move forward. I can and I will forgive. The head will cause you to doubt God. Truly let us reveal that Satan is really giving you thoughts to doubt God.

No way, no how! I WILL NEVER DOUBT GOD!!!!

Instead I reject and rebuke any and every thought that rises above the knowledge of Jesus Christ. Please trust and know that forgiveness does not happen overnight or with just one prayer. Instead, the reality of it all is that it becomes a daily decision to follow the ways of Christ. So, I press to line up my thoughts with what the word says, and I follow it, even with difficulty.

NOTE: Something that I have been doing - I say out loud: "Lord help (list the names: _____ etc.) who have hurt me. Lord bless those who cursed me. Lord help those who despitefully used me. Lord forgive them for hurting me and my family. Lord bring them to a place of repentance and save their souls. Lord give them an understanding of their actions so that it will not happen to not another person or family. **In Jesus name, Amen.**"

In doing the above I have been obedient to the word by praying for those who have despitefully used me and praying for your enemies is actually loving your enemies. This ability comes from the one who lives on the inside of my heart, the Holy Spirit.

I did not know if I had truly forgiven these individuals until I saw them face to face. When I found myself to be unexpectedly in their presence, the word came alive in my heart and I was able to speak and have no mean thoughts in my heart. Jesus did it. The word works when you work the word.

My prayer sounded like this: "Holy Spirit, lead me to where my trust is without borders. Lord help, (list the names: _____) who hurt me. Lord bless those who cursed me. Lord help those who despitefully used me. Lord forgive them for hurting me and my family. Lord bring them to a place of repentance and save their souls. Lord give them an understanding of their actions so that it will not happen to not another person or family. In Jesus name, Amen."

Chapter 15:

How Do I Do This God? God's answer to you, I have sent you: The Holy Spirit

John 14:26-27 Amplified Bible (AMP)²⁶ *But the [a]Helper (Comforter, Advocate, Intercessor— Counselor, Strengthener, Standby), the Holy Spirit, whom the Father will send in My name [in My place, to represent Me and act on My behalf], He will teach you all things. And He will help you remember everything that I have told you.*
²⁷ *Peace I leave with you; My [perfect] peace I give to you; not as the world gives do, I give to you. Do not let your heart be troubled, nor let it be afraid. [Let My perfect peace calms you in every circumstance and give you courage and strength for every challenge.]*

1 John 4:4 (AMP) *Little children (believers, dear ones), you are of God and you belong to Him and have [already] overcome them [the agents of the antichrist]; because He who is in you is greater than he (Satan) who is in the world [of sinful mankind].*

The He that the scripture is talking about is the Holy Spirit and if we allow him to do His job then there is nothing that you will ever face that is greater than the God that is on the inside of you. God is greater than any difficulty, greater than any devil, greater than any addiction. No diagnosis, no problem, no circumstance, nothing in any world that is greater than our God who makes His home in your heart.

Now the greatness cannot occur unless we obey the Holy Spirit. The Holy Spirit's job is to:

- Convict us of sin,

- Regenerate us when we are weary,

- Seal us forever as children of God,

- Teach and guides us,

- Reveal all truths,

- Comfort us,

- Give us spiritual gifts,

- Bear fruits through us,

- Empower us to do God's Holy will.

2 Timothy 3:1-5 (MSG) says, *do not be naive. There are difficult times ahead. As the end approaches, people are going to be self-absorbed, money hungry, self-promoting, stuck-up, profane,* *contemptuous of parents, crude, coarse, dog-eat-dog, unbending, slanderers, impulsively wild, savage, cynical, treacherous, ruthless, bloated windbags, addicted to lust, and allergic to God. They will make a show of religion, but behind the scenes they are animals. Stay clear of these people.*

Remember that all things work together for our good for those who are called according to His purpose. Knowing your purpose should help you to seek after God's wisdom, to seek after God's knowledge and after God's understanding.

Wisdom helps us in so many ways. It will help us to avoid great tragedies happening in our lives if we would just seek God's choices in our decisions. The renewing of our minds with the word of God will help you not to walk in disobedience, to not walk in rebellion and not have bad attitudes. Gods' purpose is for your life is to make a difference in the world. Everything that you do both big and small matters to God. Whatever bothers you bothers God. So, since He is concerned about us, why cannot we just ask God to help us with everything, not just talk to him sometimes, but talk to Him every day.

2 Corinthians 5:17 Amplified Bible (AMP)
[17] Therefore if anyone is in Christ [that is, grafted in, joined to Him by faith in Him as Savior], he is a new creature [reborn and renewed by the Holy

Spirit]; the old things [the previous moral and spiritual condition] have passed away. Behold, new things have come [because spiritual awakening brings a new life].

What better way is there to thank Jesus for His ultimate sacrifice, than by giving our lives back to Him for His glory. Do not consider it strange that God would choose to use your life to model His son's love. God will help you to change into His new masterpiece, His new creation as you begin to trust Him more and more. According to **Philippians 1:6 - *"For God has begun a good work in me, and He is well able to bring it to full completion."*** God wants you to grow in Him, allow the old things to mature you into your future. You are able to renew your mind with the Word so that old things will pass away. That thing that was declared as being old should be a reminder of the grace and mercy upon your life because you remember where He brought you from. How can we help in the process of having OLD THINGs pass away, where all things are new, fresh like a fresh wind? Accept Jesus into your heart. YOU are SAVED Forever. Pray, read, learn, and demonstrate the Word. Let the Holy Spirit direct and guide your life to Model after Jesus' heart. Submit to God and His perfect plan for your life. Choose to forgive
Choose to forget those things which bind

Choose to open your heart and your life to live a life filled with God's love.
Isaiah 43:18 says, *"Forget the former things; do not dwell on the past."*

GOD'S BEST IS THE HOLY SPIRIT

God does not want you to spend so much time and energy dwelling on the past, on mistakes, or even dwelling on disappointments. In order to fully experience God's blessings, you have to let go of those past hurts; you have to forget the former things to make room for the new. God has great new beginnings in store for you. I declare that 2013 was indeed the year of manifestation. So, let's give up old habits and people who hold us prisoner to our past and instead go forward with God toward the newness of His love, His grace and mercy, His perfect plan.

Today declare that your past is over and that you will forget the former things and receive the Holy Spirit. The Holy Spirit is your new best friend. He will teach you to obey God's will by applying the word. He reminds us of God's will. He gives us the power to live it out. Jesus' dying for me was the most He could do. Living for Him is the least I can do. Don't' criticize what you don't understand, instead ask the Holy Spirit to reveal the truth. Tell God Thank you for Jesus and tell Jesus thank you for the Holy Spirit.

THE BOX ABOVE represents your ability to offer yourself as a gift back to God.

Posterior- Don't look back except to praise God for the miracle
Lateral- Walk side by side with godly friends,
Internal- The Holy Spirit leading me,
Frontal- Press forward towards the God's purpose in my life
Lid- Honor your covering (parents, family, church leadership and mentors).

Luke 10:19 *Behold I give you the power and authority to trample on the serpents and scorpions and over all the power of the enemy and nothing shall by any means hurt you.*

God gives us the power and authority over the demonic, to ensure that the intended hurt sent our way will not harm us. Trust what God is allowing in your life, it will not take you out even though you feel like it will. Stand firm on the strong word of God. You will overcome and live to tell others about it. This too shall pass, and I will be better than when I started. I will be more confident in Christ. I will know Him more intimately. I will trust and continue to trust A Mighty God. God's love is simply amazing.

When I do not understand, He teaches me. When I am lost, He finds me. When I am confused, He guides me. He just loves me so perfectly. His love is at times so overwhelming. To think that someone could love me like that. He is totally and completely free to love me without reservation, rejection, or any restrictive provision. Jesus loves me for me. His love is such amazing gift.

If you have found yourself to be stuck and it has been so long or too long to release and forgive? Do what I did and trust again by first trusting God. For He will never do you wrong. His plans are amazing for your life. TRUST GOD TRUST your process to its COMPLETION.

TRUST the Process. I have learned that no matter how far you think you have come; it is hard to trust again once it has been shattered. TRUST ANYWAY!!! TRUST GOD. Layer upon layer we start the rebuilding of trust. Those who are closest to you are surely the ones who hurt your heart the most. Those wounds are surely the deepest because you should be safe or protected by and from the ones who are in the closest position to love you like your spouse, children, parents and our family (whatever and however you define family), it varies for each person. So, God I hurt again what do I Do? I have heard those words and my response is, say this Candace "I choose to forgive no matter how I feel, I choose to forgive and move forward."

My Pastor, Al Brice of Covenant Love Church in Fayetteville, NC has taught me the importance of making the conscious decision to forgive. This happens by depending on the power of the Holy Spirit and asking for His help to obey God by doing what He instructs me to do. Then seal it all, by enforcing the word and making it come alive in my daily living. I intentionally will not rehearse past offenses as they make me mad and are not good for my spirit. So, for those who may bring up the past, I say to them: "I have moved forward, and I choose to forgive them, and I release them. They are in God's hands." I then stand firm and I smile at what God has done. He is transforming me from the inside out. I pray that the meditations of my heart are acceptable to you my strength and my redeemer. I want to make you smile Lord.

Finally, Trusting God will take you exactly where you need to be. You may see what appears to be many delays but remember and say out loud "I TRUST GOD-the Father, I Trust God- the Son (Jesus), and I Trust God- the Holy Spirit.

May the Lord bless and keep you and have His countenance to shine upon you. May the Lord dispatch his angles before, about and around you. May God have His hedge of protection around you covering and protecting you from all harm, hurt and danger. No weapon that is formed against you shall prosper and every tongue that rises, He will condemn. Whatever you touch is blessed and prosperous for you and your family and all generations to come.

In Jesus Name, Amen.

About the Author

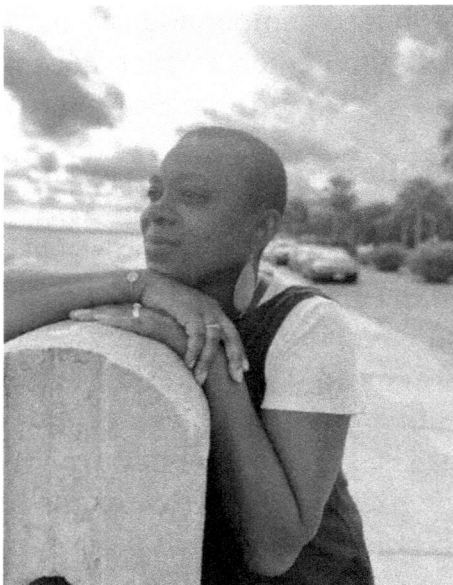

Candace B. Franklin, a native of New York City, is a wife, a mother, a daughter, a friend, a social worker and a confidant. She has a heart to help get healing jumped started by connecting the individual to the love of God. She is a servant who desires to help others restore frayed and tattered relationships with the love of Christ by using the power of prayer along with the willingness to walk daily in forgiveness. She is a light that was created by God to impact and conquer darkness by embracing the unspoken, the unrecognized and incomprehensible stain that comes from guilt, shame and pain.

Candace has a B.S. in Biology and a M.S. in Counseling Studies which allows her spiritual and natural eye the ability to see God's creation as daily inspirations that God indeed loves and cares for His people. Candace has a heart for restoring family relationships and providing encouragement in hopeless situations that are in need of a Savior. Above all of her accomplishments, Candace considers supporting her family as a number one priority for she feels that loving them entails walking in love not just at home, but also in ministry, at work and in any and every place that she finds herself in. Candace's life purpose is to encourage, inspire, lift up, empower and speak life to the young, the old and to those who are in the middle. Her desire is to serve God, love God and to be used by God!

www.wordtherapypublishing.com

"A Message That Heals"

www.ingramcontent.com/pod-product-compliance
Lightning Source LLC
LaVergne TN
LVHW011243080426
835509LV00005B/617